Frommer's™

Toronto
day BY day™

1st Edition

by Jason McBride

John Wiley & Sons Canada, Ltd.

Contents

Published by:

John Wiley & Sons Canada, Ltd.

6045 Freemont Blvd.
Mississauga, ON L5R 4J3

ISBN 978-0-470-15926-2

Editor: Gene Shannon
Production Editor: Pamela Vokey
Project Coordinator: Lynsey Stanford
Editorial Assistant: Katie Wolsley
Photo Editor: Photo Affairs, Inc.
Cartographer: Lohnes + Wright
Vice President, Publishing Services: Karen Bryan
Production by Wiley Indianapolis Composition Services

For information on our other products and services or to obtain technical support, please contact our Customer Care Department within the U.S. at 877/762-2974, outside the U.S. at 317/572-3993 or fax 317/572-4002.

Wiley also publishes its books in a variety of electronic formats. Some content that appears in print may not be available in electronic formats.

Manufactured in China

5   4   3   2   1

A Note from the Editorial Director

Organizing your time. That's what this guide is all about.

Other guides give you long lists of things to see and do and then expect you to fit the pieces together. The Day by Day guides are different. These guides tell you the best of everything, and then they show you how to see it *in the smartest, most time-efficient way*. Our authors have designed detailed itineraries organized by time, neighborhood, or special interest. And each tour comes with a bulleted map that takes you from stop to stop.

Hoping to tour Toronto's groundbreaking new works of modern architecture or dine at some of Canada's top restaurants? Planning to walk its diverse neighborhoods, visit the burgeoning gallery districts, or while away a day at the Toronto Islands? Whatever your interest or schedule, the Day by Days give you the smartest routes to follow. Not only do we take you to the top attractions, hotels, and restaurants, but we also help you access those special moments that locals get to experience—those "finds" that turn tourists into travelers.

The Day by Days are also your top choice if you're looking for one complete guide for all your travel needs. The best hotels and restaurants for every budget, the greatest shopping values, the wildest nightlife—it's all here.

Why should you trust our judgment? Because our authors personally visit each place they write about. They're an independent lot who say what they think and would never include places they wouldn't recommend to their best friends. They're also open to suggestions from readers. If you'd like to contact them, please send your comments our way at feedback@frommers.com, and we'll pass them on.

Enjoy your Day by Day guide—the most helpful travel companion you can buy. And have the trip of a lifetime.

Warm regards,

Kelly Regan

Kelly Regan, Editorial Director
Frommer's Travel Guides

About the Author

Jason McBride is a freelance writer and editor based in Toronto. He's the co-editor (with Alana Wilcox) of *uTOpia: Towards a New Toronto* and was formerly an editor at *Toronto Life* magazine. He's a frequent contributor, writing most often about pop culture, to *Toronto Life,* the *Globe and Mail, CBC Arts Online, Explore, enRoute, New York* and *The Believer.*

Acknowledgments

Thanks to my editor, Gene Shannon, for his enduring patience, good humor and surefooted guidance. To Kisha Ferguson, who very kindly led me to Gene. And, finally, to my girlfriend, Liz Sullivan, for her unwavering support and many of the the beautiful photographs that grace these pages.

An Additional Note

Please be advised that travel information is subject to change at any time—and this is especially true of prices. We therefore suggest that you write or call ahead for confirmation when making your travel plans. The authors, editors, and publisher cannot be held responsible for the experiences of readers while traveling. Your safety is important to us, however, so we encourage you to stay alert and be aware of your surroundings.

Star Ratings, Icons & Abbreviations

Every hotel, restaurant, and attraction listing in this guide has been ranked for quality, value, service, amenities, and special features using a **star-rating** system. Hotels, restaurants, attractions, shopping, and nightlife are rated on a scale of zero stars (recommended) to three stars (exceptional). In addition to the star-rating system, we also use a **kids** icon to point out the best bets for families. Within each tour, we recommend cafes, bars, or restaurants where you can take a break. Each of these stops appears in a shaded box marked with a coffee-cup-shaped bullet ☕ .

The following **abbreviations** are used for credit cards:

AE	American Express	**DISC**	Discover	**V**	Visa
DC	Diners Club	**MC**	MasterCard		

Frommers.com

Now that you have this guidebook to help you plan a great trip, visit our website at **www.frommers.com** for additional travel information on more than 4,000 destinations. We update features regularly to give you instant access to the most current trip-planning information available. At Frommers. com, you'll find scoops on the best airfares, lodging rates, and car rental bargains. You can even book your travel online through our reliable travel booking partners. Other popular features include:

- Online updates of our most popular guidebooks
- Vacation sweepstakes and contest giveaways
- Newsletters highlighting the hottest travel trends
- Podcasts, interactive maps, and up-to-the-minute events listings
- Opinionated blog entries by Arthur Frommer himself
- Online travel message boards with featured travel discussions

A Note on Prices

In the "Take a Break" and "Best Bets" sections of this book, we have used a system of dollar signs to show a range of costs for 1 night in a hotel (the price of a double-occupancy room) or the cost of an entree at a restaurant. Use the following table to decipher the dollar signs:

Cost	Hotels	Restaurants
$	under $100	under $10
$$	$100–$200	$10–$20
$$$	$200–$300	$20–$30
$$$$	$300–$400	$30–$40
$$$$$	over $400	over $40

An Invitation to the Reader

In researching this book, we discovered many wonderful places—hotels, restaurants, shops, and more. We're sure you'll find others. Please tell us about them, so we can share the information with your fellow travelers in upcoming editions. If you were disappointed with a recommendation, we'd love to know that, too. Please write to:

Frommer's Toronto Day By Day, 1st Edition
John Wiley & Sons Canada, Ltd. • 6045 Freemont Blvd. • Mississauga, ON
L5R 4J3

15 Favorite
Moments

15 Favorite **Moments**

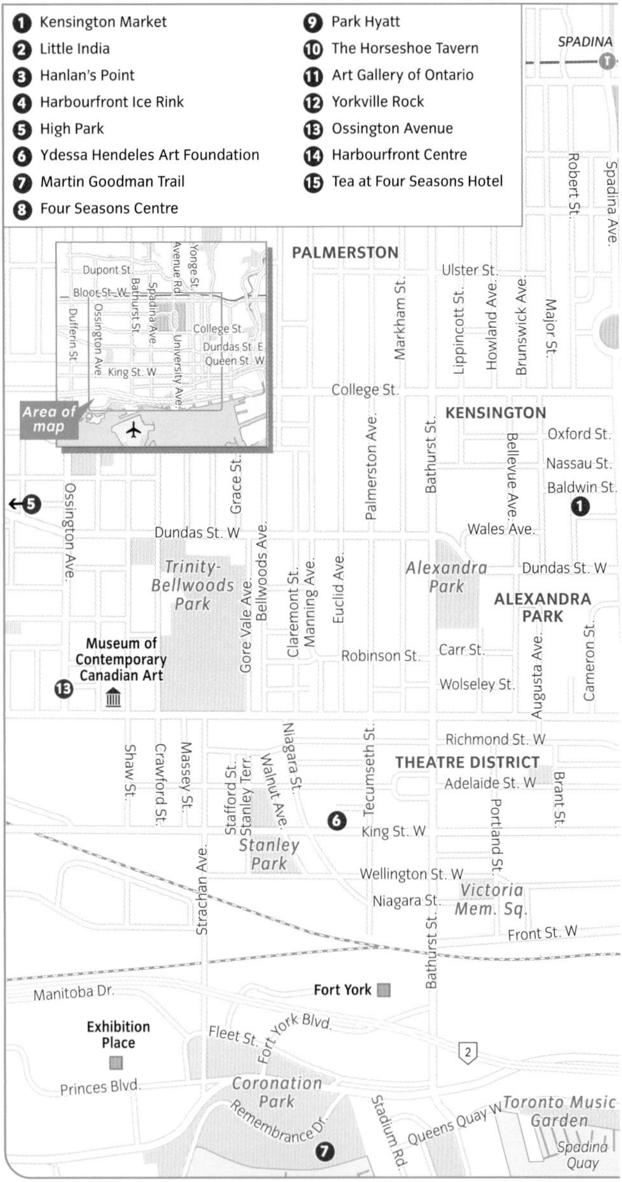

1. Kensington Market
2. Little India
3. Hanlan's Point
4. Harbourfront Ice Rink
5. High Park
6. Ydessa Hendeles Art Foundation
7. Martin Goodman Trail
8. Four Seasons Centre
9. Park Hyatt
10. The Horseshoe Tavern
11. Art Gallery of Ontario
12. Yorkville Rock
13. Ossington Avenue
14. Harbourfront Centre
15. Tea at Four Seasons Hotel

Previous page: A couple enjoys a relaxing summer afternoon on the Toronto Islands.

ANNEX

ST. GEORGE

Prince Arthur Ave.

Yorkville Ave.

Cumberland St.

12

15

9

BAY

BLOOR-YONGE

Bloor St. W

Bloor St. E

Bata Shoe Museum

Royal Ontario Museum

MUSEUM

Gardiner Museum of Ceramic Art

Hayden St.

Charles St. W

Charles St.

UNIVERSITY OF TORONTO

Devonshire Pl.

Hoskin Ave.

St. Mary St.

Inkerman St.

Isabella St.

University of Toronto Art Centre

Barnicke Gallery

Queen's Park

St. Joseph St.

St. Nicholas St.

Gloucester St.

CHURCH AND WELLESLEY

Willcocks St.

Ontario Legislature

Wellesley St. E

WELLESLEY

Maitland St.

Russell St.

Breadalbane St.

Grosvenor St.

Alexander St.

QUEEN'S PARK

Grenville St.

Wood St.

College St.

Carlton St.

COLLEGE

Orde St.

Granby St.

McGill St.

Allan Gardens

Cecil St.

Gerrard St. W

Gerrard St. E

2→

Baldwin St.

Elm St.

GARDEN DISTRICT

D'Arcy St.

CHINATOWN

11A

Edward St.

Gould St.

Sharp Centre for Design

11

ST. PATRICK

DUNDAS

Dundas St. E

Grange Ave.

Textile Museum of Canada

Mackenzie House

Sullivan St.

Grange Park

GRANGE PARK

City Hall

Eaton Centre

Phoebe St.

Bulwer St.

Old City Hall

St. Michael's Cathedral

10

OSGOODE

8

Queen St. W

QUEEN

Richmond St. W

Temperance St.

Lombard St.

ST. ANDREW

King St. W

St. James Cathedral

St. James Park

KING

King St. E

Mercer St.

Colborne St.

Wellington St. W

Wellington St. E

FINANCIAL DISTRICT

Royal Bank Plaza

Front St. E

CBC

Front St. W

UNION

The Esplanade

Convention Center

Station St. Union Station

Rogers Centre

CN Tower

Bremner Blvd.

Air Canada Centre

2

Bremner Blvd.

11A

Lake Shore Blvd. W

Queens Quay W

HARBOURFRONT

4

3↓

Maple Leaf Quays

14

🚇 Subway Stop

🏛 Museum

⬜ Point of Interest

0   1/4 mi

0   0.25 km

Canada's largest city has at last shed its reputation as a dull, repressed metropolis. What locals and visitors alike have discovered is an ever-expanding city with a remarkably diverse population; a vibrant cultural landscape; unique, ethnic neighborhoods overflowing with charming shops and architecture; and a culinary scene that's one of the finest in North America. Below are my 15 favorite things to do in Toronto.

Selecting fresh fruit at Kensington Market.

❶ Shopping for a picnic in Kensington Market. The Market's always evolving, but one constant is the good, eclectic food at the various stalls and shops. Pick up cheese, meat, and fruit (and maybe an empanada or patty) and head to a nearby park (Queen's Park is good or the many at the University of Toronto) for a picnic. *See p 32.*

❷ Strolling through Little India. A perfect summer evening on this 6-block stretch of Gerrard Street East consists of munching on fresh barbecued corn, window shopping for saris, and taking a break for a cooling lassi. A walk down narrow, funky Craven Road makes for a nice detour. *See p 33.*

❸ Sunbathing at Hanlan's Point. If you're here in the summer, a trip to the Toronto Islands is a must. This secluded beach, part of which is clothing optional, boasts silky sand and relatively warm water—yes, you can swim in it—and is far from the maddening crowd that descends on Centre Island. *See p 95.*

❹ Ice skating at Harbourfront. Harbourfront's Natrel Ice Rink is the city's largest and on a crisp winter's night, there's no better place to be. You'll feel like you're skating on the adjacent Lake Ontario—which you practically are. *See p 11.*

❺ Hiking in High Park. Toronto's largest park is home to a myriad of natural delights—from an eccentric zoo to allotment gardens and unspoiled hiking trails. It's a sublime sanctuary—and a great place to disappear for an hour or two. *See p 90.*

⑥ Reveling in Ydessa Hendeles' art collection. The city's preeminent—and most eccentric—art collector puts on a new show only once a year (or two). And you can spend just as long trying to unravel the meaning of the way she's curated, arranged, and displayed the diverse work (ranging from antique dolls to cutting-edge video art). *See p 42.*

⑦ Biking along the Martin Goodman Trail. This trail runs along Lake Ontario for over 322km (200 miles) and Toronto sits smack-dab in the middle of it. Get on at Sunnyside in the west and take a leisurely ride, about an hour, out to the beaches in the east. It's a unique perspective that few tourists experience. *See p 98.*

⑧ Enjoying free classical music at the Four Seasons Centre. The soul-stirring Opera House offers a great program of free lunchtime concerts. Brown-bag it and grab one of the 154 seats in the Richard Bradshaw Amphitheatre. *See p 25.*

⑨ Sipping shiraz on the Park Hyatt patio. This was once a popular hangout for the city's literati. While these days, your drinking buddies will more likely be lawyers, the

Cycling on the Martin Goodman Trail.

elegance of this tiny L-shaped patio—and its stunning views—never goes out of style. *See p 123.*

⑩ Rocking out at the Horseshoe. The city's most venerable saloon, now 60 years old, continues to hop. Grab a bottle of Labatt 50 and discover a new band everyone will be talking about a year from now. *See p 137.*

⑪ Strolling the length of the Galleria Italia at the AGO. This long, sun-drenched gallery, at the front of the Frank Gehry–redesigned Art Gallery of Ontario, is a sculpture unto itself—made up of light, glass, and

Diners enjoy authentic Indian cuisine amid Little India's vibrant colors.

The beautifully crafted and designed Galleria Italia at the AGO.

Douglas fir wood. Strolling its length is an extraordinary experience, both meditative and awe inspiring. It feels like some kind of spacecraft dreamed up by indigenous peoples. *See p 41.*

⓬ **People-watching on the rock in Yorkville Park.** Park yourself here—on this billion-year-old, 650-ton rock in the middle of Yorkville—on the first day of spring and watch the passing parade of the überrich, the überstylish, and, sometimes, the überfamous. Oh, and lots of tourists. *See p 57.*

⓭ **Barhopping along Ossington Avenue.** Ossington Avenue is currently the city's trendiest nightlife real estate. Weekends are strictly amateur hour, however. Visit on a Wednesday or Thursday night if you want to clink glasses with the neighborhood's artistic denizens. *See p 116.*

⓮ **Sampling free music at Harbourfront.** All summer long, Harbourfront Centre presents a dizzying array of tunes—from world to electronica to emerging Canadian bands—at no charge. And there's always lots of scrumptious international food being sold in nearby stalls. *See p 11.*

⓯ **Enjoying afternoon tea at the Four Seasons.** Get a small (and delicious) taste of Toronto's British heritage, with a modern twist. The luxurious Lobby Bar at this celebrity haunt serves a classic high tea—with fresh-baked scones and cucumber-and-mint sammies—but juices things up by pairing teas with prosecco and martinis. *See p 57.* ●

The Horseshoe Tavern is the place to go to catch talented, up-and-coming bands.

1

The Best **Full-Day Tours**

The Best in **One Day**

ANNEX
SPADINA
Prince Arthur Ave.
ST. GEORGE
Yorkville Ave.
Cumberland St.
Avenue Rd.
BAY

Dupont St.
Bloor St. W
Avenue Rd.
Yonge St.
Spadina St.
Bathurst St.
Dufferin St.
Ossington Ave.
College St.
Dundas St. E
Queen St. E
King St. W

Area of map

0   1/4 mi
0   0.25 km

Bloor St. W   5
Bata Shoe Museum
MUSEUM
Devonshire Pl.
Gardiner Museum of Ceramic Art
Charles St. W
Bay St.

UNIVERSITY OF TORONTO
Hoskin Ave.
Queen's Park Crescent W
St. Joseph St.

University of Toronto Art Centre
Queen's Park
Barnicke Gallery
Ontario Legislature
St. George St.
Willcocks St.
Russell St.

Major St.

QUEEN'S PARK

College St.

KENSINGTON
Oxford St.
Nassau St.
Baldwin St.
Wales Ave.
Bellevue Ave.
Augusta Ave.
Spadina Ave.
Huron St.
Ross St.
Cecil St.
Henry St.
McCaul St.
Murray St.
Orde St.
University Ave.
Gerrard St. W
Elizabeth St.
Bay St.

D'Arcy St.
CHINATOWN
11A
ST. PATRICK

Baldwin St.
Beverley St.

Markham St.
Bathurst St.
Alexandra Park
ALEXANDRA PARK
Augusta Ave.
Cameron St.
Dundas St. W
Grange Ave.
Art Gallery of Ontario
Grange Park
Sharp Centre for Design
St. Patrick St.
Simcoe St.
Textile Museum of Canada

Carr St.
Wolseley St.
Sullivan St.
Phoebe St.
Bulwer St.
Soho St.
GRANGE PARK
Campbell House
City Hall
Queen St. W
OSGOODE

Richmond St. W
THEATRE DISTRICT
Camden St.
Adelaide St. W
Brant St.
Spadina Ave.
Peter St.
Widmer St.
John Ave.
Duncan St.
Simcoe St.
York St.
Richmond St. W
St. ANDREW
King St. W
University Ave.

Mercer St.
Clarence Square
Blue Jays Wy.
Wellington St. W
Bay St.
FINANCIAL DISTRICT
UNION

Subway Stop
Museum
Point of Interest

Front St. W
CBC
Front St. W
Convention Center
Station St.
Union Station
Air Canada Centre
Rogers Centre
Bremner Blvd.
Bremner Blvd.
2

Lake Shore Blvd. W
York St.
Queens Quay W
HARBOURFRONT
Maple Leaf Quays

1 Yorkville
2 Royal Ontario Museum
3 Queen's Park
4 The Gallery Grill
5 University of Toronto
6 Queen Street West
7 CN Tower
8 Harbourfront Centre

Previous page: The CN Tower is the world's second tallest freestanding structure.

Toronto's a sprawling metropolis, the fifth largest in North America in fact, but you can still get a good sense of its charms by taking this "greatest hits" tour. Going right through the heart of the city, and unfolding in a straightforward, easy-to-follow way, this stroll takes you from the famed Yorkville neighborhood to Toronto's constantly evolving waterfront. START: **Bay Station.**

1 ★★ **kids** **Yorkville.** With its quaint Victorian houses and cobblestone streets, Yorkville has long been one of Toronto's most desirable neighborhoods—and dramatically emblematic of the city's evolution. In the 1960s and 1970s, this was hippie central, with coffeehouses home to local musical lights like Joni Mitchell and Gordon Lightfoot. As the counterculture moved south to Queen Street West, upscale boutiques moved in and now the area is notable for its exclusive shopping, luxurious hotels and condos, and, during film festival time in September, celeb spotting. Kids love clambering over the giant granite rock that sits at the western edge of a unique park on Cumberland Street. ⏲ *30 min. Subway: Bay.*

2 ★★★ **kids** **Royal Ontario Museum.** In 2008, the Royal Ontario Museum completed a dramatic makeover, adding a controversial glass-and-metal addition dubbed "The Crystal" that

The Royal Ontario Museum has an impressive dinosaur collection.

transformed this staid stalwart into an exhilarating new destination. Naysayers might grumble about the cost of the renovation ($320 million) and architect Daniel Libeskind's eccentric design, but tell that to the thousands of visitors that line up outside every morning to take in the museum's 6 million natural history and world culture objects—from

People-watching on a patio in Toronto's upscale Yorkville neighborhood.

native kayaks to the ever-popular dinosaur collection. ⏱ *2 hr. 100 Queen's Park.* ☎ *416/586-8000. www.rom.on.ca. Admission $22 adults, $19 seniors and students, $15 children, free for children 2 and under. Free admission every Wed 4:30–5:30pm. Mon–Thurs 10am–5:30pm, Fri 10am–9:30pm, Sat–Sun 10am–5:30pm. Subway: Museum.*

❸ ★ **Queen's Park.** Toronto is the capital of Ontario and the provincial parliament buildings, opened in 1893, occupy prime real estate in the center of the city. The Legislative Building itself was built in the Richardsonian Romanesque style, characterized by dramatic arches and massive stone walls, here made of Ontario sandstone. Various tours of the building's history, art, and architecture are available, many of them free. Political junkies can watch feisty parliamentary sessions from the public galleries (check the website for a calendar). ⏱ *1 hr. Legislative Assembly of Ontario, Queen's Park.* ☎ *416/325-7500. www.ontla.on.ca. Free admission. Summer (Victoria Day weekend to Labor Day) daily 9am–4pm; fall, winter, and spring, Mon–Fri 10am–4pm. Subway: Queen's Park.*

❹ ★★★ **The Gallery Grill.** One of the most elegant lunch spots in town, this University of Toronto gem offers a setting—Gothic ceilings, stained-glass windows—as sumptuous as its largely organic, locally sourced menu. A leisurely lunch (accompanied by a guarapo mojito) is ideal but quick soups, salads, and fresh juices are also available. *7 Hart House Circle.* ☎ *416/978-2445. $$.*

❺ ★★ **University of Toronto.** Canada's largest university (in terms of enrollment), the University of Toronto has three different campuses, two of which are located in the suburbs. The downtown St. George campus features plenty of handsome late-19th-century Gothic revival and Romanesque architecture, while less comely brutalist buildings include the enormous, peacock-shaped Robarts Library, nicknamed "Fort Book." Some highlights: Soldiers' Tower, a monument to students who lost their lives in war; Hart House, a multipurpose student center (featuring the excellent Justina M. Barnicke Gallery); and Philosopher's Walk, a secluded pathway behind the law and music faculties. The school continues to expand

Inside Type Books on Queen Street West.

aggressively, with the addition of space-age structures like the Norman Foster–designed Leslie L. Dan Pharmacy Building. ⏱ *60 min. Begin at Hart House, 7 Hart House Circle. Subway: Museum or St. George.*

6 ★★ Queen Street West. Once the city's most notorious bohemian enclave—home to a vibrant punk and art scene in the early 1980s—the strip's gentrification has it today resembling a trendy outdoor mall. But even with skyrocketing rents and the overwhelming presence of clothing chains like H&M and Zara, a bit of the old Queen West character survives. Students from the nearby Ontario College of Art and Design continue to haunt Black Market, a vintage T-shirt shop; the Rex has morphed from a dingy dive to the city's premiere jazz club; and aging rockers still hold court at the Horseshoe Tavern. ⏱ *30 min. Begin at Queen and Bathurst and head east.*

7 ★★ kids CN Tower. No longer the world's tallest freestanding structure—that distinction now belongs to the United Arab Emirates' Burj Dubai—this 553m (1,815-ft) communications tower nonetheless remains the city's most famous emblem (and a great way to orient yourself). Much is made of the height—the nerveracking Glass Floor, through which you can see all the way to street level, was built to withstand the weight of 14 large hippos; the Sky Pod features a 360-degree perspective of the entire city (and, on a clear day, you can see Niagara Falls, about 129 kilometers [80 miles] away); the restaurant, 360, is more famous for its views than its food. Brand-new, glass-bottomed elevators rocket you to these attractions in less than a minute. ⏱ *30 min. 301 Front St. W. ☎ 416/868-6937. www.cntower.ca. Admission Total Tower Experience (Look Out, Glass Floor, Sky Pod,*

At 553 meters (1,815 feet) high, the CN Tower offers an unbeatable view of the city.

movie and motion theater ride) $33, all ages; Observation Sky Pod Experience (Look Out, Glass Floor, Sky Pod) $27 adults, $25 seniors, $21 children 4–12; Observation Experience (Look Out and Glass Floor) $22 adults, $20 seniors, $15 children 4–12. Subway: Union.

8 ★★★ kids Harbourfront Centre. Toronto's waterfront development has been slow and controversial, but this sprawling complex is its crown jewel. Located right on the lip of the lake and a stone's throw from many downtown hotels, Harbourfront is host to dozens of ethnic cultural, art, and music festivals throughout the year, as well as free outdoor movies, concerts, kids' activities, art shows, and theatrical extravaganzas. In winter, bring your skates (or rent them here)—Harbourfront's also home to the city's largest outdoor ice rink. ⏱ *1 hr. 235 Queens Quay West. ☎ 416/973-4600. www.harbourfront centre.com. Free admission. Subway: Union (take either the 509 Exhibition or 510 Spadina streetcar west from inside Union Station and disembark on the third stop, Lower Simcoe St.).*

The Best Full-Day Tours

The Best in **Two Days**

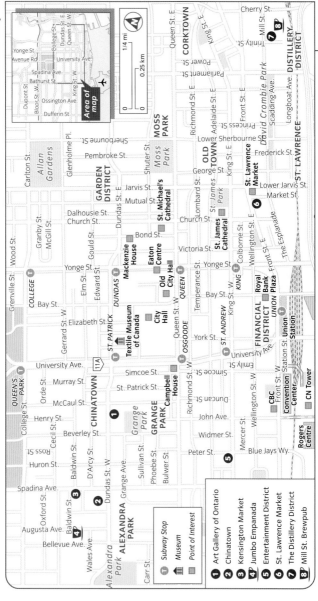

Area of map

1/4 mi

0.25 km

CORKTOWN
Cherry St.
King St. E
Queen St. E
Power St.
Parliament St.
Trinity St.
Mill St.
DISTILLERY DISTRICT
7
8

MOSS PARK
Sherbourne St.
Pembroke St.
Glenholme Pl.
Carlton St.
Allan Gardens
GARDEN DISTRICT
Shuter St.
Moss Park
Richmond St. E
Lower Sherbourne St.
OLD TOWN
Adelaide St. E
Princess St.
Front St. E
David Crombie Park
Scadding Ave.
Longboat Ave.
ST. LAWRENCE

Dalhousie St.
Church St.
Jarvis St. E
Mutual St.
St. Michael's Cathedral
George St.
Lombard St.
King St. E
St. James Park
St. Lawrence Market
6
Lower Jarvis St.
Frederick St.
Market St.

Granby St.
McGill St.
Wood St.
Bond St.
Gould St.
Mackenzie House
Eaton Centre
Old City Hall
DUNDAS
QUEEN
Victoria St.
Church St.
St. James Cathedral
Colborne St.
Yonge St.
Wellington St. E
Front St. E
The Esplanade

Grenville St.
Bay St.
Elm St.
Edward St.
Yonge St.
COLLEGE
ST. PATRICK
Textile Museum of Canada
City Hall
Queen St. W
OSGOODE
York St.
ST. ANDREW
Temperance St.
Bay St. W
KING
FINANCIAL DISTRICT
Royal Bank Plaza
UNION Station
Union Station

Gerrard St. W
Bay St. W
Elizabeth St.
University Ave.
11A
QUEEN'S PARK
Murray St.
Simcoe St.
St. Patrick St.
Richmond St. W
Emily St.
University Ave.
Wellington St. W
Station St.
CBC
Front St. W
Convention Center
CN Tower

College St.
Orde St.
McCaul St.
Henry St.
Beverley St.
Ross St.
Cecil St.
Huron St.
CHINATOWN
Grange Park
GRANGE PARK
Campbell House
1
Duncan St.
John Ave.
Widmer St.
Peter St.
Mercer St.
Blue Jays Wy.
5
Rogers Centre

Spadina Ave.
Oxford St.
Augusta Ave.
Bellevue Ave.
Baldwin St.
D'Arcy St.
Sullivan St.
Phoebe St.
Bulwer St.
ALEXANDRA PARK
Grange Ave.
Dundas St. W
2
3
4

Alexandra Park
Wales Ave.
Carr St.

Inset map labels:
College St.
Dundas St.
Queen St.
Yonge St.
Avenue Rd
University Ave.
Spadina Ave.
Bathurst St.
Dupont St.
Bloor St. W
Ossington Ave.
Dufferin St.
King St. W

Legend:
- Subway Stop
- Museum
- Point of Interest

1 Art Gallery of Ontario
2 Chinatown
3 Kensington Market
4 Jumbo Empanada
5 Entertainment District
6 St. Lawrence Market
7 The Distillery District
8 Mill St. Brewpub

With the top tourist spots out of the way, it's time for an intimate, but no less exhaustive, look at some of Toronto's more compelling nooks. This sprawling tour begins with art and ends with design, and, in between, explores some of the city's most bustling, colorful markets. START: **St. Patrick Station.**

The renovated AGO is Canada's first Frank Gehry building.

1 ★★★ **Art Gallery of Ontario.** When the scaffolding came off the Art Gallery of Ontario in November 2008, it was like the wrapping paper had been ripped from an amazing birthday gift. The city—and the country, in fact—finally had its own Frank Gehry building (the architect was born here) and it did not disappoint. And with 110 separate galleries and 4,000 works of art on view, there's something—a Warhol or perhaps an aboriginal boomerang—for everyone. ⏱ *2 hr. 317 Dundas St. W.* ☎ *877/225-4246. www.ago. net. Admission $18 adults, $15 seniors, $10 students and youth 6–12, free for children 5 and under. Free admission Wed 6–8pm. Tues & Sat–Sun 10am–5:30pm; Wed–Fri 10am–8:30pm. Subway: St. Patrick.*

2 ★★ **Chinatown.** Toronto's Chinese population is so immense that the city actually has four Chinatowns. But the one that formed in the late 19th century around Dundas and Spadina is the oldest, biggest, and most centrally located. Like many Chinatowns, however, Toronto's is a blend of several East Asian cultures and you'll find restaurants and shops that cater as well to the Vietnamese, Korean, and Thai communities. There are dazzling supermarkets, to be sure, but just outside them, wizened grandmothers sit on sidewalks, hawking herbs grown in their own backyard gardens. The place never stops buzzing—in the early morning, you can find stalls full of ridiculously cheap exotic produce, fresh fish, and

Chinatown is home to a variety of East Asian shops and restaurants.

The St. Lawrence Market offers fresh, top-quality local produce year-round.

baked goods; at night, many of the restaurants stay open until the wee hours. 🕐 *30 min. Begin at College St. and Spadina Ave. and head south.*

❸ ★★★ Kensington Market.

The ever-evolving Market (as it's typically known) has morphed, with each successive wave of immigration, from a Jewish ghetto—in the 1930s, about 30 synagogues dotted the environs—into one of the city's most vibrant neighborhoods. It's now a kind of multicultural, bohemian utopia. The hub of the Market is its abundant fresh produce stalls, butchers, and cheese stores, but these are surrounded by eclectic cafes, restaurants, bars, vintage clothing stores, and bookshops. Gentrification, a constant fear of locals, has been a reasonably gentle process, with almost all the retail remaining fiercely independent and unique. 🕐 *45 min. Begin at Spadina and Baldwin and head west.*

☕★★ Jumbo Empanada. The

name says it all—this friendly, family-run spot serves up fat, filling, and authentic empanadas, a kind of South American sandwich made of puff pastry and stuffed with veggies, chicken, or beef. Seating's limited but in warmer months the small patio out front is perfect for people-watching. *245 Augusta Ave.* ☎ *416/977-0056. $.*

❺ Entertainment District. This

sprawling section of downtown includes most of the city's pro sports stadiums—the Air Canada and Rogers centres—as well as the major commercial theaters, the Royal Alex and Princess of Wales; the Hockey Hall of Fame; the Canadian Broadcasting Corporation's headquarters (and museum); and, by 2010 or so, the Bell Lightbox, the much-anticipated future home of the Toronto International Film Festival. At night, the nightclubs that dominate the adjacent blocks swell with suburban kids (and the cops that police them). Given the area's abundant hotels and lively restaurants and pubs, the streets are often clogged with sightseers and business folk, but a stroll along the main King Street drag is always energizing. ⏱ *45 min. Subway: St. Andrew.*

❻ ★ St. Lawrence Market.

Once the site of Toronto's City Hall, this handsome building was renovated in 1899 and converted into a cavernous food market. Another renovation in the 1970s gave the basement more retail outlets and turned the second floor into a gallery, housing the municipal government's decorative and fine art collection. Today, the market thrives, with hundreds of retailers selling meat, fish, produce, baked goods, and prepared foods. The North Market, across the street, becomes a Farmers' Market on Saturday and the Antique Market, with 80 different dealers, on Sunday. ⏱ *1 hr. 92 Front St. E. ☎ 416/392-7120. www.stlawrencemarket.com. South Market Tues–Thurs 8am–6pm, Fri 8am–7pm, Sat 5am–5pm; Farmers' Market Sat from 5am; Antique Market Sun dawn–5pm. Subway: Union (from there, walk east along Front St. for 3 blocks).*

❼ ★★ The Distillery District.

A kind of culture and heritage mall, the Distillery was once exactly what its name indicates—the Gooderham and Worts Distillery, purveyor of fine whiskey and rum from 1831 until 1990. When the factory closed up shop, the haunting Victorian buildings became a favorite location for film crews. In 2003, the area was transformed into a charming, pedestrian-only complex dedicated to art, design, and entertainment. The impressive architecture now forms a backdrop for artists' studios and galleries, exclusive shops,

Studios and galleries in the pedestrian-friendly Distillery District.

restaurants, and the Young Centre for the Performing Arts, home of the renowned Soulpepper Theatre Company. ⏱ *1 hr. 55 Mill St. ☎ 416/364-1177. www.thedistillery district.com. Subway: Castle Frank (from there, take the 65A Parliament St. bus south to Front, walk 2 blocks south to Mill St.).*

❽ ★★ Mill St. Brewpub. This

557sq. m (6,000-sq.-ft.) brewery produces handcrafted ales and lagers, incorporating many of their signature brews in an extensive lunch and dinner menu. The Original Organic Lager's a crowd pleaser, but the syrupy Coffee Porter (made with beans from Balzac's Café (see p 27), around the corner) will keep you going all night long. *55 Mill St., Bldg 63. ☎ 416/681-0338. $$.*

The Best in **Three Days**

CHRISTIE

BATHURST

1 High Park
2 Roncesvalles Village
3 Granowska's
4 Little Italy
5 The Toronto Islands
6 Yonge-Dundas Square
7 The Danforth
8 Kalyvia

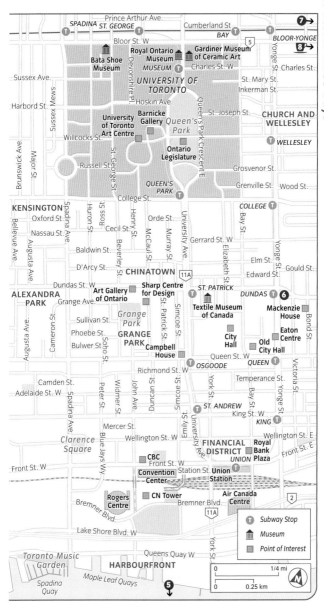

Prince Arthur Ave.
SPADINA **ST. GEORGE** Cumberland St *BAY* *BLOOR-YONGE*
Bloor St. W
Royal Ontario Museum Gardiner Museum of Ceramic Art
Bata Shoe Museum *MUSEUM* Charles St. W
Sussex Ave. St. Mary St.
UNIVERSITY OF TORONTO Inkerman St.
Harbord St. Hoskin Ave. St. Joseph St. **CHURCH AND WELLESLEY**
Barnicke Gallery *Queen's Park*
University of Toronto Art Centre *WELLESLEY*
Willcocks St.
Ontario Legislature Grosvenor St.
Russell St. Grenville St. Wood St.
QUEEN'S PARK
College St.
KENSINGTON *COLLEGE*
Oxford St. Orde St.
Nassau St. Cecil St. Gerrard St. W Elm St.
Baldwin St. Edward St. Gould St.
D'Arcy St.
Dundas St. W **CHINATOWN** [11A]
ALEXANDRA PARK Art Gallery of Ontario Sharp Centre for Design *ST. PATRICK* *DUNDAS*
Grange Ave. Textile Museum of Canada Mackenzie House
Sullivan St. *Grange Park* City Hall Old City Hall Eaton Centre
Phoebe St. **GRANGE PARK**
Bulwer St. Campbell House Queen St. W *QUEEN*
Richmond St. W *OSGOODE*
Camden St. Temperance St.
Adelaide St. W
King St. W
Mercer St. *ST. ANDREW* *KING*
Clarence Square Wellington St. W **FINANCIAL DISTRICT** Royal Bank Plaza Wellington St. E
Front St. E
CBC *UNION*
Front St. W Station St. Union Station
Convention Center
Front St. W
CN Tower Air Canada Centre
Rogers Centre Bremner Blvd.
Bremner Blvd. [11A]
Lake Shore Blvd. W
Toronto Music Garden Queens Quay W
HARBOURFRONT
Spadina Quay Maple Leaf Quays

Subway Stop
Museum
Point of Interest

0   1/4 mi
0   0.25 km

Toronto is often described as a "city of neighborhoods"— which is another way of saying it's one of the most multicultural metropolises in the world. While much of its ethnic diversity can be found in the suburbs, the downtown districts reflect earlier waves of immigration. This wide-ranging tour introduces several of these neighborhoods, as well as some of the city's most beautiful outdoor attractions. START: **High Park Station.**

Travel Tip

For this tour, which covers a lot of distance, pick up a Toronto Transit Commission (TTC) day pass for $10 at any subway station. It gets you unlimited one-day travel on all regular TTC services.

1 ★★★ kids **High Park.** Toronto's equivalent of Central Park is a bit less central than New York's landmark, but no less bucolic. Almost 162 hectares (400 acres) in size, about a third of High Park remains in its pristine, natural state (featuring oak savannahs and various rare plants). The rest has been given over to gardens, bike and hiking trails, recreational facilities, a fish-stocked pond, and a small zoo. Free walking tours are conducted every second and fourth Sunday (starting at 10:30am) and last 90 minutes. ⏱ *1 hr. 1873 Bloor St. W.* ☎ *416/392-1748. www.toronto.ca/ parks/highpark.htm. Subway: High Park.*

Walk east from the southeastern gate at High Park Boulevard to Roncesvalles Avenue.

2 ★★ **Roncesvalles Village.** Just east of High Park, the colorful strip from Dundas West to Queen West is home to Toronto's tight-knit Polish community, with several prominent Polish Catholic churches, delis, and shops dotting the avenue. A flower-draped memorial statue of Pope John Paul II stands at the corner of Roncesvalles and Fern avenues. In recent years, some of the strip's Polish character has been supplanted (or enhanced, depending on your view) by trendy shops, bistros, and cafes, as young families (and their SUV-size strollers) move into the neighborhood. ⏱ *30 min. Subway: Dundas West (begin at Roncesvalles Ave. and Howard Park and head south).*

High Park's idyllic scenery attracts nature-lovers from all parts of the city.

Little Italy's patios opened in the '60s and remain popular today.

3 ★ Granowska's. Most famous for having provided pastries to Pope John Paul II on his first visit to Canada, this 33-year-old bakery serves up predictable Polish fare (jelly donuts, pirogi), made with great love, family recipes, and natural ingredients. *175 Roncesvalles Ave.* ☎ *416/533-7755. $.*

At Roncesvalles Avenue and Howard Park Boulevard take the 506 College streetcar east to Grace Street.

4 ★★ Little Italy. Toronto reportedly has the largest Italian community outside of Italy itself, with huge numbers of Italians settling in the College and Clinton area in the early part of the 20th century. In the 1960s, this was the first neighborhood to permit patio service, initiating a lively cafe culture that still flourishes today. With subsequent waves of Portuguese immigrants and boho hipsters transforming College (as it's popularly known), its charm can now be chalked up to the numerous multiethnic restaurants and funky shops. At night it becomes, for better or worse, a miniclubland, the strip overflowing with suburban weekend warriors. ⏱ *30 min. Subway: Queen's Park (from there, take 506 Carlton streetcar west to Clinton).*

Walk west to Spadina, take 510 streetcar south to Queens Quay. Walk a block farther west to Bay Street and follow the signs for the ferry terminal.

5 ★★★ kids The Toronto Islands. Just a short ferry ride away from the foot of Bay Street lies a Toronto that too few tourists see. This small archipelago was developed by the city as a park in the 1950s and today includes beaches, bike paths, an artists' retreat, an amusement park, and several homes (262 houses are clustered on the eastern tip, the remainder of a once-thriving, prepark residential community). Centre Island

The Toronto Islands offer the best views of the city's skyline.

Yonge-Dundas Square often hosts free performances and festivals.

is typically overcrowded on summer weekends—ferry lines can stretch out along Queens Quay—so you're better off taking your picnic basket to the more secluded Hanlan's Point. ⏱ *3 hr. Subway: Union (from there, take the 509 Harbourfront streetcar to the Bay and Queens Quay stop). Ferries run about every 15 minutes during the summer but schedules vary; check www.toronto.ca/parks/ island for more information or call 416/392-8193. Round-trip fare $6 adults, $4 seniors and children 15–19, $3 children 3–14, free for children under 2.*

6 Yonge-Dundas Square. The intersection of Yonge and Dundas is reportedly Toronto's number-one visitor destination. Too bad it's still such a shabby spot. A sort of Times Square wannabe—neon drenched, loud, hemmed in by the Eaton Centre and Toronto Life Square—the public square only occasionally possesses the energy and excitement the city envisioned when it unveiled it in 2003. Still, Yonge-Dundas often hosts interesting free performances, festivals, and celebrations, everything from concerts by Fall Out Boy to the Toronto African Dance Festival. The

city's first "pedestrian scramble"— allowing pedestrians to cross at the same time from all directions— opened at the intersection in 2008. ⏱ *15 min. Subway: Dundas.*

7 The Danforth. This long stretch of Danforth Avenue is North America's largest Greek neighborhood, officially established in 1972. Naturally, you'll find numerous restaurants specializing in souvlakia and spanakopita—and the requisite cries of "Opa!"—but the Greektown strip is also home to trendy boutiques and cafes catering to the Prius-driving residents of Riverdale, an affluent, left-leaning neighborhood to the south. The Krinos Taste of the Danforth Festival, an immense, annual celebration of all things Hellenic, takes place every August. ⏱ *30 min. Subway: Chester.*

8 Kalyvia. Grab a spot on the sunny patio, order a horiatiki (traditional Greek salad) or appetizer plate (overflowing with authentic taramasalata and hummus) and you'd swear you're in a taverna in Sparti, the owners' birthplace. *420 Danforth Ave.* ☎ *416/406-6666. $.* ●

Cultural Toronto

1 Gardiner Museum	**6** Four Seasons Centre		
2 Royal Ontario Museum	**7** The Distillery District		
3 L'Espresso Bar Mercurio	**8** Balzac's Coffee Roastery		
4 Bata Shoe Museum	**9** Harbourfront Centre		
5 Spadina Museum House and Historic Garden	**10** The Gladstone Hotel		

● Subway Stop
■ Point of Interest

```
0          1/4 mi
0     0.25 km
```

Previous page: The Ontario College of Art and Design's Sharp Centre for Design.

In recent years, Toronto has enjoyed a long-overdue cultural renaissance. Many of the city's old institutions (including the Royal Ontario Museum and the Art Gallery of Ontario) have undergone massive renovations and upgrades, while exciting new exhibition and performance spaces—most notably, a state-of-the-art opera house—have greatly transformed the look and feel of the city. Move over Montreal, Toronto is now the country's real artistic capital. START: **Museum Station.**

Part of the impressive ceramics collection at the Gardiner Museum.

❶ ★ Gardiner Museum.
Devoted entirely to the study and display of ceramics, this beguiling museum was overhauled, expanded, and reopened in 2006 to great acclaim. With an additional 1,301 sq. m (14,000 sq. ft.), the museum has successfully attracted new audiences to a 3,000-piece collection that includes Asian and European porcelain, unique scent bottles, and contemporary Canadian teapots. Every Friday and Saturday, a $10 drop-in clay class lets visitors get their hands dirty. ⏱ *1 hr. 111 Queen's Park.* ☎ *416/586-8080. www. gardinermuseum. on.ca. Admission $12 adults, $8 seniors, $6 students, free for children 11 and under, ½ price Fri 4–9pm. Mon–Thurs 10am–6pm, Fri 10am–9pm, Sat–Sun 10am–5pm. Subway: Museum.*

❷ ★★ kids Royal Ontario Museum. Canada's largest natural history museum is now even bigger, with an additional six galleries open after a 2008 expansion. The World Culture galleries include Asian, African, and ancient art, artifacts from Canada's earliest First Nations societies (including Sitting Bull's headdress, locked up for the last 30 years), and a textile and costume gallery

A cultural relic on display at the ROM.

Author! Author!

Many of Canada's most renowned novelists and poets live here, and it's not uncommon to see Margaret Atwood at the Annex farmers' market or Michael Ondaatje cruising through Cabbagetown. Some sense of the city's writerly history can be gained by visiting Toronto's literary landmarks, including **Matt Cohen Park** (Spadina and Bloor) and **Gwendolyn MacEwen Park** (Walmer and Bloor), both situated near the late authors' former homes; or the **Al Purdy** statue in Queen's Park. A new plaque near the Bloor Viaduct heralds a moment from Ondaatje's novel *In the Skin of a Lion*. The tiny lane behind Innis College at the University of Toronto commemorates **bpNichol**, the late avant-gardist (one of his whimsical poems has been etched into the concrete). Nichol's press, the venerable, 40-year-old **Coach House Books** (401 Huron St., on bpNichol Lane), is still going strong and welcomes curious visitors.

with more outfits than a *Gossip Girl* marathon. The Natural History galleries house even more crowd pleasers: the Bat Cave, the Age of Dinosaurs, and an interactive biodiversity gallery. In the summer, the museum conducts ROMWalks, free guided tours of different city neighborhoods and architecture. ⏲ *2 hr. See p 9,* ❷.

❸ L'Espresso Bar Mercurio.
The patio of this trendy yet traditional Italian cafe provides surprising refuge from bustling Bloor. (You'd never know there is a grad student residence above you.) Naturally, espresso is the order of the day, perfect alongside panini made with in-house-baked bread. *321 Bloor St. W.* ☎ *416/585-2233. $.*

❹ **Bata Shoe Museum.** This is, perhaps, Carrie Bradshaw's idea of heaven, an eccentric, four-story museum that houses hundreds of, yes, shoes—from ancient Egyptian sandals to Japanese bear fur shoes, and Marilyn

Monroe's pumps. The permanent collection goes back 4,500 years and revolving exhibitions highlight the development of ballet flats and the craft of native footwear. ⏲ *1 hr. 327 Bloor St. W.* ☎ *416/979-7799. www. batashoemuseum.ca. Admission $12 adults, $10 seniors, $6 students, $4 children, free for children 4 and under, Pay What You Can (PWYC) Thurs 5–8pm. Mon–Wed and Fri–Sat 10am–5pm, Thurs 10am–8pm, Sun noon–5pm. Subway: St. George.*

❺ ★ **Spadina Museum House and Historic Garden.** Get a good glimpse of old (read, 19th-century) Toronto culture with a stop at the historic home of financier James Austin. Four generations lived here, as the stately, 50-room

A Cherokee moccasin from the Bata Shoe Museum.

An audience at The Four Seasons Centre enjoys a free afternoon concert.

wonder morphed from Victorian country estate to Edwardian city manse. In 1978, one of Austin's descendants donated the house and its contents to the city. Guided tours of the home's interiors (containing all the original Arts and Crafts and Art Deco furnishings and decorations) are conducted on the quarter-hour. ⏲ *1 hr. 285 Spadina Rd.* ☎ *416/392-6910. Admission $7.60, $5.50 seniors and youth 13–18, $4.50 children 6–12, free for children 5 and under. Jan–Mar Sat–Sun noon–5pm; Apr to Labor Day Tues–Sun noon–5pm; Sept–Dec* *Tues–Fri noon–4pm, Sat–Sun noon–5pm; Christmas and New Year's Eve noon–3pm. Subway: Dupont (from there, walk north to the Baldwin Steps at Spadina and Davenport; the museum is at the top of the steps).*

❻ ★★★ Four Seasons Centre. Having long clamored for an opera house, Toronto finally got one in 2006. Boasting impeccable sightlines and acoustics—even in the nosebleeds—this Diamond and Schmitt–designed, European-style hall is a permanent home to the Canadian Opera Company and a regular performance venue for the National

The Zeidler Effect

The sharp eyed will notice that one particular dynasty—the Zeidler family—has had quite an effect on cultural Toronto. Patriarch Eb, who immigrated to Canada from Germany in 1951, is one of the city's preeminent architects and developers, the mind behind both the Eaton Centre (p 87) and Ontario Place (p 39). His eldest daughter Margie transformed an old factory at Richmond and Spadina into the creative hot spot now known as 401 Richmond (p 60) and her sister, Christina, turned the Gladstone Hotel into the city's hippest crash pad and art center.

The Young Centre for the Performing Arts in the Distillery District.

Ballet. Free lunchtime concerts (classical, jazz, and world music) are held in the sunny, 154-seat Richard Bradshaw Amphitheatre. Hour-long tours ($7) run most Saturdays at noon. ⏱ *1 hr. 145 Queen St. W.* ☎ *416/363-6671. www.coc.ca. Tickets $30–$290. Subway: Osgoode.*

❼ ★★ The Distillery District. Some call it the "hippest address in town," and while that's debatable, this unique cluster of 45 converted industrial buildings is still downright cool. The Young Centre, the Distillery's most spectacular space, has expanded to become a multidisciplinary home for other festivals and programs, something akin to New York City's Lincoln Center. The Distillery's galleries are diverse and immense (Clark-Faria and Corkin are just two of the most illustrious); the performance spaces are state-of-the-art, and a virtual village of artisans is housed in the Case Goods Warehouse—from goldsmiths to ceramicists and sculptors. ⏱ *1 hr. See p 15,* ❼.

Festival of Festivals

Toronto's extraordinary ethnic heritage is never more visible than in the summer, when just about every neighborhood sponsors a weekend festival of some kind, complete with food and entertainment that celebrate a particular culture. Some highlights: the Taste of Little Italy (late June), the Krinos Taste of the Danforth (Aug), the Toronto Chinatown Festival (late Aug), and the big daddy of them all, Caribana (July–Aug). *See our Special Events calendar, p 162.*

8 Balzac's Coffee Roastery.
The Distillery branch of this indie coffee chain (the original's in Stratford, another's in Liberty Village) is a cozy spot in winter and, in summer, it's a treat to enjoy their fairtrade, roasted-on-the-premises java at one of the outside picnic tables. *55 Mill St., Bldg. 60.* ☎ *416/207-1709. $.*

9 Harbourfront Centre. If you can't get enough crafts, head down to Harbourfront and tour the Craft Studio. Open to the public, the studio provides equipment and studios to emerging metalsmiths, glass blowers, and textile artists. Lectures, workshops, and master classes are also held throughout the year. Bounty, the studio's retail arm, is an adorable shop full of contemporary Canadian crafts and art. ⏱ *30 min. See p 38,* **8**.

10 ★★★ The Gladstone Hotel.
This was a 120-year-old derelict flophouse until it was bought and converted by the cherished Zeidler family (see "The Zeidler Effect," above) in 2005. Book a room here—there are 37, each designed and furnished by local artists—and you may never want to leave. Day and night, the hip hotel hosts some of

Balzac's offers fair-trade, fresh-roasted coffee in a beautifully adorned room.

the most eclectic, exciting cultural events in the city, many of them free—from poetry readings to bluegrass performances, book launches to art shows. Guests who like to sing can duck into the Melody Bar for its famed weekend karaoke. ⏱ *30 min. 1214 Queen St. W.* ☎ *416/531-4635. www.gladstonehotel.com. Subway: Osgoode (from there, take the 501 streetcar west to Queen and Gladstone). See p 146.*

The Gladstone Hotel is a cultural hub for art shows, concerts, and readings.

Culinary Toronto

St. Clair Ave. W

ST. CLAIR WEST 🔵

Winston Churchill Park

Benson Ave. W ❺

Hocken Ave.

Tyrrel Ave.

Wychwood St.

Christie St.

Davenport Rd.

Bathurst St.

Area of map

✈

🔵 Subway Stop

◾ Point of Interest

Hammond Pl.

DUPONT 🔵

Dupont St.

Vermont Ave.

Howland Ave.

Spadina Ave.

Olive Ave.

Follis Ave.

Barton Ave.

Clinton St.

Christie St.

Markham St.

Bathurst St.

Ossington Ave.

Concord Ave.

Dovercourt Park

Shanly St.

Dovercourt Rd.

Christie Pits Park

BATHURST **SPADINA** 🔵

DUFFERIN 🔵

OSSINGTON 🔵

CHRISTIE 🔵

5

Bloor St. W

Manning Ave.

Euclid Ave.

Palmerston Ave.

Lennox St.

Sussex Ave.

Bickford Park

Harbord St.

5

❸

Harbord St.

PALMERSTON

Lippincott St.

Howland Ave.

Brunswick Ave.

Robert St.

Shaw St.

Roxton Rd.

Ulster St.

Clinton St.

Markham St.

Spadina Ave.

Havelock St.

Rusholme Rd.

Dovercourt Rd.

Delaware Ave.

Concord Ave.

Ossington Ave.

Shannon St.

George Ben Park

LITTLE ITALY

College St.

KENSINGTON

Bathurst St.

Bellevue Ave.

Augusta Ave.

Nassau St. ❻

Dundas St. W

Harrison St.

Crawford St.

Grace St.

Dundas St. W

Alexandra Park

Ryerson Ave.

Dufferin St.

Gladstone Ave.

Lisgar St.

Dovercourt St.

Argyle St.

Trinity-Bellwoods Park

Museum of Contemporary Canadian Art 🏛

ALEXANDRA PARK

Bellwoods Ave.

Claremont St.

Robinson St.

Palmerston Ave.

Richmond St. W

Queen St. W

❹

THEATRE DISTRICT

Adelaide St. W

Massey St.

Crawford St.

Shaw St.

Niagara St.

Spadina Ave.

King St. W

Allan Lamport Stadium Park

King St. W

Stanley Park

Victoria Mem. Sq.

Fraser Ave.

Dufferin St.

❷

Strachan Ave.

Bathurst St.

Front St. W

← ❶

2

Manitoba Dr.

Fort York ◾

2

1 Cheese Boutique
2 Atelier Thuet
3 Dufferin Grove Park
4 The Red Tea Box
5 Artscape
   Wychwood Barns
6 Kensington Market
7 Cumbrae's
8 Soma
9 Yonge and
   Summerhill LCBO
10 Little India

J ust as it's impossible to define Canadian cuisine—no, pancakes and maple syrup don't cut it—it's impossible to define Toronto's cuisine. That's a good thing. With such a multicultural population, the culinary landscape is huge and you can find, without much effort, virtually every type of dish, ingredient, and restaurant imaginable. Accordingly, this tour ranges quite widely, from the west of the city to the far east—but there's plenty of sustenance along the way. START: **Runnymede Station.**

❶ ★★★ **Cheese Boutique.** Hands down, this is Toronto's greatest, most eccentric, cheese shop (just ask any chef) and well worth the trip to the city's western limits. Now 40 years old, and still in the proud hands of the Pristine family, this is the gourmet grocer that first introduced Torontonians to brie and it continues to guide them through the wonderful, complex worlds of cheese, olive oil, California truffles, and rare peppercorns. ⏱ *45 min. 45 Ripley Ave.* ☎ *416/762-6292. Subway: Runnymede (from there, take the 77 Swansea bus south to South Kingsway and Ripley).*

❷ ★★ **Atelier Thuet.** Alsace-born bad-boy chef Marc Thuet opened this Liberty Village bakery/butcher/bistro initially to sell his trademark charcuterie and rare cheeses stored in his custom-designed vault. But the

shelves also groan with other delectable delights: aged organic beef, Canadian and Russian caviars, truffled chicken pot pies, pots of jam, and Thuet's artisanal breads—the ingredients for a very exclusive (and pricey) picnic. The gourmet shop doubles as a fully functioning restaurant, with a kitchen open until midnight and an excellent brunch. ⏱ *30 min. 171 East Liberty St., unit 153–155.* ☎ *416/603-2777. Subway: St. Andrew (from there, take the 504 King streetcar west to Atlantic and walk south to Liberty).*

❸ ★★ **Dufferin Grove Park.** Food is a very important part of this friendly, community-minded hippie haven. Every Thursday from 3 until 7pm, year-round, a large part of the 5.7-hectare (14-acre) park is transformed into a bustling organic farmers' market (see "Field to Table,"

Atelier Thuet offers fine meats, rare cheeses, and fresh-baked artisanal breads.

The farmers' market at Dufferin Grove Park raises money for community programs.

below). Two wood ovens are used communally to turn out the breads and pizza sold in the Zamboni Café. (Do-it-yourself bakers can use the residual heat after 3pm on Thurs or purchase sourdough starter for home baking.) In summer, a food cart dispenses hot dogs, salads, cookies, and coffee by the Cob Courtyard. Food sales help fund recreation and art programs in the park. 45 min. 875 Dufferin St. 416/392-0913. www.dufferin park.ca. Subway: Dufferin.

★ **The Red Tea Box.** A more traditional high tea might be found at the Four Seasons but this adorable tea shop offers the funky, Queen West version. In the secluded back patio behind the shop, you can sample 32 different tea blends while also enjoying cakes or a savory bento-box lunch. *696 Queen St. W.* 416/203-8882. *$.*

Field to Table

As in many culinary capitals, fresh and local are foodie buzzwords in Toronto. And each year, the city's network of farmers' markets grows ever larger, with new neighborhoods getting their own weekly fix of bounty straight from Ontario's fields and orchards. At last count, there were roughly 30 such markets spread out across the Greater Toronto Area (GTA), the vast majority of which are open from spring to fall with a couple (Dufferin Grove, Artscape Wychwood Barns) open all year long. The number and type of stalls vary (with products as diverse as fresh strawberries, smoked whitefish, and wild mushrooms), but all are staffed by knowledgeable growers and provide perfect picnic fixings. Check www.greenbeltfresh.ca or call 416/960-0001 for times and locations.

The Red Tea Box carries a wide variety of teas and elaborately decorated cakes.

5 ★★ Artscape Wychwood Barns. This wonderful ecofriendly community center—a set of converted Toronto Transit Commission streetcar garages—serves many functions: art studios, park, event and exhibition space. Its most compelling complex, however, is the so-called Green Barn, operated by the Stop Community Food Centre. Consisting of a greenhouse, protected community gardens, and an outdoor bake oven, it also provides classes and workshops on sustainable food and nutrition. ⏱ *30 min. 76 Wychwood Ave.*

Cumbrae's specializes in premium, locally raised meats.

☎ *416/392-1038. Subway: Christie (from there, take the 126 Christie bus north and get off just south of St. Clair).*

6 ★★★ Kensington Market. Tucked between Little Italy and Chinatown, the mercurial Market occupies prime foodie real estate. Fine fishmongers, butchers, and cheese shops do a brisk business. Spice shops, produce stalls, and specialty markets (Latin American products, especially, are plentiful) round out the culinary offerings. New cafes seem to open everyday and some of the city's best coffee (see "Bean Counters," below) can be found here, at I Deal and Moonbeam. Vegans will drool over the sandwiches at the expanded Urban Herbivore. The whimsical Good Egg sells unique books and accessories (David Shrigley tea towels anyone?) that will brighten your kitchen back home. ⏱ *1 hr. See p 14,* **3**.

7 Cumbrae's. Espousing a "farm-to-fork" ethos, the city's best butcher specializes in premium, naturally raised beef, lamb, pork, and poultry—all raised in Ontario, antibiotic and hormone free. Fine prepared foods (salads, meat pies) are also available. ⏱ *15 min. 481 Church St.* ☎ *416/923-5600. Subway: Wellesley.*

Bean Counters

Forget the Starbucks debate of 2001—Toronto is now awash in superior independent java joints and aficionados are *very* particular about what kind of coffee fills their morning mug. The revolution's broken out everywhere. Obsessive **Manic Coffee** (426 College St.; ☎ 416/966-3888), home of the $15 cup, buys its beans direct from growers, bypassing even fair-trade dealers. The **Common** (1071 College St.; ☎ 416/546-7789) is cozy and serves up excellent Americanos. East-enders adore **Mercury Espresso Bar** (915 Queen St. E.; ☎ 647/435-4779) and its splendid organic cappuccinos. I'm partial to the smooth Princess of Darkness blend at the grungy indie chain **I Deal Coffee** (84 Nassau St.; ☎ 416/364-7700).

8 Soma. Just take a deep breath upon entering this sweet shop and you'll know why chocolate's called the food of the gods. The back-room lab turns out handmade confections—from heirloom, chili-flavored bars to candied Australian ginger hand dipped in Venezuelan chocolate. In colder months, a mug of Mayan hot chocolate is a must. *55 Mill St., Bldg. 48. ☎ 416/815-7662. $.*

9 Yonge and Summerhill LCBO. Liquor is almost exclusively sold in stores operated by the government-run Liquor Control Board of Ontario (LCBO). Their beautiful, multi-roomed Toronto flagship, housed in a former railway station, is the most attractive and best stocked. ⏱ *30 min. 10 Scrivener Sq. ☎ 416/922-0403. Subway: Summerhill.*

10 ★ Little India. This bright 6-block stretch of Gerrard Street East, between Greenwood and Coxwell, swells with around 200 Indian, Pakistani, Afghani, and Sri Lankan shops and restaurants. Of course, this is the go-to place for Indian cuisine—everything from *dosas* (pancakes) to *tikka*, all of it at reasonable prices—and exotic fruit, spices, dozens of different chutneys, and cooking utensils can be found at B.J. Supermarket and Kohinoor Foods. In the summer, a special treat is the fresh barbecued corn, slathered in butter, lime, and spice, sold outside many storefronts. ⏱ *1 hr. Subway: Greenwood (from there, take the 31 Greenwood bus south to Gerrard St. E.).*

Soma's mouth-watering offerings.

Almond Cluster dipped in Venezuelan dark chocolate

Toronto with Kids

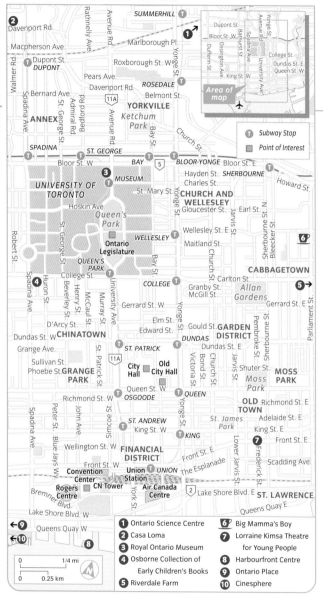

1. Ontario Science Centre
2. Casa Loma
3. Royal Ontario Museum
4. Osborne Collection of Early Children's Books
5. Riverdale Farm
6. Big Mamma's Boy
7. Lorraine Kimsa Theatre for Young People
8. Harbourfront Centre
9. Ontario Place
10. Cinesphere

Given its relative youth and occasional awkwardness, Toronto has been called a teenager of a city. True or not—every year, the city becomes more sophisticated—it definitely offers plenty of fun for kids of all ages, from the amazing delights of the Science Centre to the cuddly creatures at Riverdale Farm. Even getting around town can be a treat—a ride at the front of a subway or streetcar can keep little ones amused for a surprisingly long time. This tour starts toward the top of the city and proceeds straight down to the lake. START: **Eglinton Station.**

❶ ★★★ **Ontario Science Centre.** This interactive science museum has been delighting young and old with its exhibits—more than 800 of them, spread throughout 10 halls—of technology, biology, and physics since 1969. You could literally spend the whole day here (and your kids, who will be having a blast, might insist on it). A 3-year, $47-million renovation brought the museum into the 21st century, with an expansion of KidSpark, a learning center and playground where junior Einsteins eight and under can build a roller coaster, cook a meal, or explore the mysteries of water. Older kids can test their skills in the Sport Hall; wander through a real, live rain forest; or go on a virtual airplane flight. The recently opened Teluscape takes things outside, emphasizing the

The Ontario Science Centre provides learning activities for all ages.

museum's relationship to the neighboring Don Valley, and features, at its center, artist Steve Mann's FUNtain, a beguiling, hands-on sound and water sculpture. ⏱ *2 hr. 770 Don Mills Rd.* ☎ *416/696-1000. www. ontariosciencecentre.ca. Admission $18 adults, $14 seniors and youth 13–17, $11 children 4–12, free for children 2 and under. Open daily 10am–5pm. Subway: Eglinton (from there, take the 34 Eglinton bus east to Don Mills Rd.).*

❷ **Casa Loma.** While not immediately obvious as a children's attraction, imaginative kids get a lot out of this, Toronto's only castle. Built between 1911 and 1914 by wealthy financier Sir Henry Pellatt, this homage to the knights and castles of yore served as his private home until overwhelming debt forced him to abandon it in 1924. The city took over and transformed it into a tourist attraction in 1937. Adults can soak up the palatial design and furnishings while adventurous little ones investigate the stables, secret passages, and 244m (800-ft.) tunnel, or, depending on the time of the year, take in a Wizard Workshop or check out Sleeping Beauty's Enchanted Castle. ⏱ *1 hr. 1 Austin Terrace* ☎ *416/923-1171. www. casaloma.org. Admission $17 adults, $11 seniors and youth 14–17, $9.25 children 4–13. Open daily 9:30am–5pm (gardens only open May–Oct). Subway: Dupont (from there, walk north 2 blocks on Spadina Ave. and*

Today's Babysitter

Every year, Today's Parent KidSummer (www.kidsummer.com) serves as the city's biggest unofficial babysitter. Sponsoring and organizing events, classes, and camps for teens and tots across the city, the program includes such diverse activities as animation workshops at the National Film Board, berry picking, art gallery visits, TV station tours, and baseball games. Many activities are free for kids 2 to 12 (with small fees for adults), while others, with capacity limits, require preregistration (check the website for details).

climb the Baldwin Steps at Spadina and Davenport).

❸ ★★★ Royal Ontario Museum.
With the Royal Ontario Museum bigger and better than ever before, kids can't get enough of the place—especially the dinosaurs. There are 50 dino specimens, including 25 fully mounted skeletons, representing 120 different types of dinosaurs. Gordo, the museum's 27m (90-ft.) *Barosaurus* skeleton, is the largest dinosaur on permanent display in Canada. Videos and other interactive displays provide helpful and fun background. ROMkids is a regular program for children 16 and under and includes special sleepover nights, expanded weekend activities,

and an exclusive Explorer's Club. 🕐 *1 hr. See p 9,* ❷.

❹ ★ Osborne Collection of Early Children's Books.
Budding bookworms will fall in love with this remarkable trove of kid lit, some of the rarer items going as far back as 2000 B.C. Other highlights include a 14th-century manuscript of Aesop's fables, Florence Nightingale's childhood library, and original art by Maurice Sendak. Special exhibits have included spotlights on Edward Gorey and pop-up books. 🕐 *30 min. Toronto Public Library, Lillian H. Smith Branch, 239 College St.* ☎ *416/393-7753. Free admission. Mon–Fri 10am–6pm, Sat 9am–5pm. Subway: Queen's Park.*

Studying dinosaur specimens at the ROM.

Family-friendly Riverdale Farm offers educational activities year-round.

5 ★★ Riverdale Farm. Located in the heart of Cabbagetown, this adorable, city-operated working farm consists of 3 hectares (7.5 acres) of herb-and-vegetable gardens, ponds, woods, and animal paddocks full of cows, horses, sheep, pigs, and rabbits. Much of the farm serves as a simple petting zoo—one much more conveniently located than the immense Toronto Zoo, out in the burbs—and there are also many programs and events designed to teach kids about animal husbandry and farm life (eggs are collected, cows milked). Parents will enjoy the refreshments made and served in the Farm Kitchen and the shop, which sells handicrafts, preserves, books, and soaps. In colder months, the Meeting House offers puzzles, games, and a play barn. ⏱ *45 min. 201 Winchester St. ☎ 416/392-6794. Free admission. Open daily 9am–5pm. Subway: Castle Frank (from there, take the 65 Parliament St. bus south to Winchester and walk east to the end of the street).*

6 Big Mamma's Boy. This friendly neighborhood restaurant serves up traditional pizzas and pastas, made largely from locally grown ingredients. Parents of kids with allergies will love the abundant gluten and dairy-free choices. *554 Parliament St. ☎ 416/927-1593. $$.*

Screen Tots

Generally speaking, the Toronto International Film Festival (TIFF) is off-limits to young people, so TIFF decided in 1997 to start a film fest exclusively for children and teens. The **Sprockets International Film Festival for Children** (www.sprockets.ca) shows international shorts and features for kids ages 3 and up, running the gamut from cartoons to foreign-language experimental work. The movies tend to be smart and sophisticated—no *Kung Fu Panda* here—so adults won't get fidgety. The fest's been so successful that, although it runs for only a week in April, the Sprockets Globetrotter series now screens a different new film every month (see the website for details).

Performers onstage at the Lorraine Kimsa Theatre for Young People.

❼ ★ Lorraine Kimsa Theatre for Young People. A professional drama and theater school for children, this 43-year-old institution has produced some of the country's most renowned plays for young audiences. There are generally eight productions a season, a good mix of international classics and contemporary Canadian work, geared toward audiences from pre-schoolers to high school students. While the drama program obviously requires a longer time commitment, weekend workshops for teens are offered throughout the year in musical theater, stage combat, and more. ⏱ 1 hr. 165 Front St. E. ☎ 416/862-2222. www.lktyp.ca. Tickets $20 adults, $15 children 1–18. Subway: Sherbourne (from there, take the Sherbourne bus to Front).

❽ ★★ Harbourfront Centre. Kids and families get the deluxe treatment here, with programming and events geared specifically to them year-round. HarbourKIDS is an ongoing program of indoor and outdoor fun, including free movies, skating (both ice and, inside, on

Thrills, Chills & Spills

Canada's Wonderland, the city's biggest and best amusement park, lies in the northern suburbs, but is a fairly quick trip from downtown (GO Transit buses run regularly from the Yorkdale and York Mills subway stations). The park's home to an 8-hectare (20-acre) water park, more than 200 attractions, and 65 rides, including the Behemoth, Canada's tallest and fastest roller coaster. Admission runs from $30 to $54.

If you haven't had your fill of cotton candy, head to the Canadian National Exhibition, known to locals as "the Ex." The 18-day, 130-year-old fair—held annually in the last two weeks of August—is the largest in Canada and features a huge, bustling midway with more than 50 rides and attractions. ☎ 416/393-6000; www.theex.com. General admission runs from $11 to $15 and a family pass is $45.

skateboards), arts and crafts, and sports activities. In winter, the 25-year-old Natrel ice rink, right next to the lake, is Toronto's largest outdoor rink and there's good hot chocolate in the adjoining Lakeside Eats cafe. ⏱ *1 hr. See p 27,* **9**.

9 Ontario Place. While this amusement park has seen better days—the decor's increasingly drab, the abundance of corporate sponsorship garish—there's nowhere better on a steamy summer day than its water park, Soak City. Lines for the slides can take forever but the interactive Waterplay area's fountains and squirt guns provide plenty of cool relief. The park's other attractions include replica hot air balloons, pedal boats, a miniputt course, and a huge arcade. Events featuring TV and book characters like Bob the Builder run throughout the day. The Ontario Place Guaranteed Weather policy ensures that rain won't ruin the fun.

At Harbourfront, children's activities range from arts and crafts to ice skating.

Ontario Place offers a "guaranteed weather" policy for rainy days.

⏱ *2 hr. 955 Lakeshore Blvd. W.* ☎ *416/314-9900. www.ontario place.com. Admission to grounds $17.75 ages 6–64, $11.75 seniors and children 4–5, free for children 3 and under; Play All Day Pass $33.50 ages 6–64, $17.75 seniors and children 4–5, free for children 3 and under. Mid-May to Labor Day daily 10am–dusk; evening events close later. Closed early Sept to early May. Subway: Union (from there, take the 509 Harbourfront streetcar to Exhibition Place, then walk south over the Lakeshore Bridge).*

10 Cinesphere. This IMAX theater, opened in 1971, is part of the Ontario Place complex and is billed as the world's first permanent IMAX. Whatever that distinction means, this is nonetheless the largest screen in the GTA (24m wide×18m high/80 ft.×60 ft.) with a theater that seats 752 people. The usual IMAX fare is on tap, from heart-stopping films about dinosaurs to jaw droppers about the Amazon. ⏱ *1 hr. Viewers choice ticket $8 (other ticket prices and packages vary). First screening daily 10:15am. Ontario Place grounds admission is required for entry to Cinesphere.*

Toronto for Art Lovers

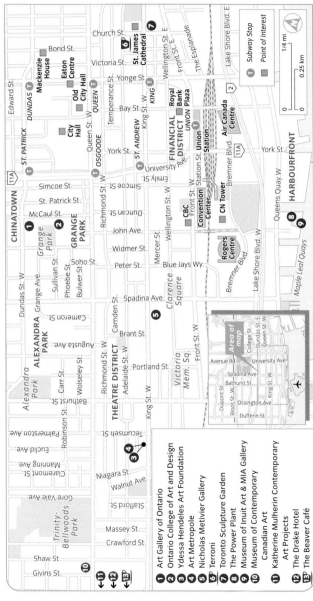

Church St.

St. James Cathedral

Bond St.

Mackenzie House

Eaton Centre

Victoria St.

Old City Hall

DUNDAS

Yonge St

Temperance St.

QUEEN

City Hall

Bay St. W

Royal Bank Plaza

FINANCIAL DISTRICT

King St. W

UNION Plaza

Air Canada Centre

Queen St. W

OSGOODE

York St. W

ST ANDREW

Union Station

Bremner Blvd.

Wellington St. E

Front St. E

The Esplanade

Lake Shore Blvd. E

York St.

HARBOURFRONT

ST. PATRICK

University Ave.

Emily St.

Station St.

Edward St.

Simcoe St.

St. Patrick St.

McCaul St.

CHINATOWN

Grange Park

GRANGE PARK

Richmond St. W

Simcoe St.

Duncan St.

John Ave.

Widmer St.

Peter St.

Mercer St.

Wellington St. W

CBC

Convention Center

Front St. W

CN Tower

Queens Quay W

Bremner Blvd.

Rogers Centre

Lake Shore Blvd. W

Maple Leaf Quays

Dundas St. W

Grange Ave.

Sullivan St.

Phoebe St.

Bulwer St.

Soho St.

Cameron St.

Camden St.

Spadina Ave.

Blue Jays Wy.

Clarence Square

Brant St.

ALEXANDRA PARK

Augusta Ave.

Portland St.

Victoria Mem. Sq.

Front St. W

Alexandra Park

Carr St.

Wolseley St.

Adelaide St. W

THEATRE DISTRICT

King St. W

Bathurst St.

Robinson St.

Tecumseh St.

Palmerston Ave

Euclid Ave

Manning Ave

Claremont St.

Niagara St.

Walnut Ave.

Gore Vale Ave.

Stafford St.

Trinity-Bellwoods Park

Massey St.

Crawford St.

Shaw St.

Givins St.

1. Art Gallery of Ontario
2. Ontario College of Art and Design
3. Ydessa Hendeles Art Foundation
4. Art Metropole
5. Nicholas Metivier Gallery
6. Terroni
7. Toronto Sculpture Garden
8. The Power Plant
9. Museum of Inuit Art & MIA Gallery
10. Museum of Contemporary Canadian Art
11. Katherine Mulherin Contemporary Art Projects
12. The Drake Hotel
13. The Beaver Café

Subway Stop

Point of Interest

1/4 mi

0.25 km

Area of map

College St.

Dundas St. E

Queen St. W

Avenue Rd

University Ave.

Spadina Ave

Bathurst St

King St. W

Dupont St

Bloor St. W

Ossington Ave.

Dufferin St

Contemporary art has, in recent years, been characterized by cross-pollination and this is particularly true in Toronto, the birthplace of such multimedia superstars as Michael Snow and General Idea. An exciting array of artwork, much of it combining sculpture, installation, and performance, is being produced here today—and there's a corresponding diversity of galleries and spaces in which to see it. It's best to take this tour any day but Monday, when many galleries are closed. START: **St. Patrick Station.**

① ★★★ Art Gallery of Ontario.
A recent, much-hyped redesign, courtesy of Frank Gehry, has breathed much-needed life into this stalwart, truly transforming it into a world-class gallery that's both intimate and immense. There's a new restaurant (named, what else, Frank), an expanded retail shop, and, of course, brand-new exhibition spaces and freshly acquired art. Even the buttery light feels new, flooding the Galleria Italia, a promenade overlooking Dundas Street, and streaming into the fourth and fifth floors dedicated to contemporary art. The public can now enjoy the hundreds of works, including Rubens' *The Massacre of the Innocents* (previously unavailable due to lack of exhibition space), donated by the gallery's great benefactor, the late financier Kenneth Thomson or David Altmejd's startling new

sculpture installation, *The Index,* which represented Canada at the Venice Biennial in 2007. The genius of the gallery is its curatorial attention, allowing each of the 4,200 works on display—an Emily Carr painting next to, say, a Rodney Graham photograph—to comment on each other and their own place in art history. ⏱ *2 hr. See p 13,* ❶.

② ★ Ontario College of Art and Design. The centerpiece of the country's largest art school is an eye-catching, eccentric structure, designed by Will Alsop, that's officially called the Sharp Centre for Design. Unofficially, the building, a large black-and-white box, suspended on 12, multicolored legs nine stories above the school's main campus, has been called the Tabletop or a crossword puzzle on stilts. But love it or hate it, the Sharp Centre's given

OCAD's striking "crossword puzzle on stilts" has transformed Toronto's skyline.

Art Attack

Taking a cue from the success of events in Paris and Montreal, Toronto launched its version of Nuit Blanche (www.scotiabanknuit blanche.ca)—the "free all-night contemporary art thing" in 2006. It was an unqualified success, with 425,000 people venturing out to enjoy strange, sweet, and surprising artworks located all across the city—from houses draped in gigantic tea cozies to sound installation in the subway. Subsequent editions haven't been met with as much enthusiasm—the crowds have grown, of course, and with them the expectations—but it's an annual fall event that still gets the whole city buzzing. And downing a lot of caffeine.

the skyline some necessary wit and color and, in summer, the giant box provides plenty of shade for picnicking students (although you'll have to be a student to explore the building's interior). ⏲ *10 min. 100 McCaul St.* ☎ *416/977-6000. Subway: St. Patrick.*

❸ ★★★ **Ydessa Hendeles Art Foundation.** This is the most mysterious and beguiling gallery in the city, the personal vision of one obsessive collector with an amazing eye. Each of Hendeles' shows—some of which run for years—consists of pleasantly strange configurations of objects, photographs, paintings, and sculpture, all from her personal

collection. The gallery, housed in a forbidding former uniform factory, is dramatically and dimly lit, nearly silent, and open to the public only 5 hours a week. ⏲ *1 hr. 778 King St. W.* ☎ *416/413-9400. Admission $3. Open Sat noon–5pm. Subway: St. Andrew (from there, take the 504 King streetcar west to Tecumseth).*

❹ ★★ **Art Metropole.** Next door to Hendeles is this nifty shop/gallery specializing in books by and about artists, as well as limited edition, multimedia multiples. Founded by General Idea in 1974, it currently sells well-priced work by many of Toronto's emerging conceptual artists as well as international

The Nicholas Metivier Gallery shows fine contemporary art and photography.

The Toronto Sculpture Garden exhibits inventive pieces like this Mushroom Studio.

bigwigs. ⏱ *30 min. 788 King St. W. ☎ 416/703-4400. www.artmetro pole.com. Free admission. Tues–Fri 11am–6pm, Sat noon–5pm. Subway: St. Andrew (from there, take the 504 King streetcar west to Tecumseth).*

❺ Nicholas Metivier Gallery.

This warm, two-story gallery showcases many of the city's finest contemporary artists and photographers. Major shows have featured the likes of Joanne Tod, John Scott, and Max Dean. Edward Burtynsky is probably the most renowned such figure; his stunning, nearly abstract photographs of industrial wastelands can be found in magazines and museums around the world. ⏱ *20 min. 451 King St. W. ☎ 416/205-0900. www.metiviergallery.com. Free admission. Tues–Sat 10am–6pm. Subway: St. Andrew.*

❻ Terroni. While a very full meal can be had at this famed trattoria, you can also grab a quick pizza or panini. The emphasis is on traditional Southern Italian ingredients and techniques; substitutions are verboten and don't even think of asking for a Diet Coke. *57A Adelaide St. ☎ 416/203-3093. $$.*

❼ ★ Toronto Sculpture Garden.

Sandwiched between two Georgian buildings built in the 1840s, this tiny parkette is home to an ever-changing exhibition of contemporary public art, the more whimsical the better. Past artworks have included *Mushroom Studio,* a witty homage to Californian roadside attractions, as well as pieces by esteemed local artists Derek Sullivan and Luis Jacob. ⏱ *10 min. 115 King St. E. ☎ 416/515-9658. www.toronto sculpturegarden.com. Free admission. Daily 8am–dusk. Subway: King.*

❽ The Power Plant. Considered by many to be Canada's foremost contemporary art institute, the Power Plant has a somewhat checkered past. Curators and directors have come and gone—although the current administration has been in power for a few years—and the reception of many recent shows has been mixed. Nonetheless, the gallery's large, inviting spaces have given Torontonians their first glimpse of international stars like Francesco Vezzoli and Harrell Fletcher, while also championing local artists. The regular lecture series and free tours (part of the Sunday Scene program) are helpful and informative. ⏱ *45 min. 231 Queens Quay W. ☎ 416/973-4949. www.thepowerplant.org. Admission*

The Katharine Mulherin gallery is a longtime promoter of the city's younger, edgier artists.

$5 adults, $3 seniors and students, free for children and on Wed 5–8pm. Tues–Sun noon–6pm, Wed noon–8pm. Subway: Union (take either the 509 Exhibition or 510 Spadina streetcar west from inside Union Station and disembark on the third stop, Lower Simcoe St.).

⑨ Museum of Inuit Art & MIA Gallery. Founded by two former teachers from Baffin Island, this museum is devoted to contemporary and ancient Inuit art and includes the city's largest whale-bone sculpture. The adjoining gallery sells work (sculptures, ceramics, prints, and wall hangings) from both accomplished and emerging artists from over 25 Northern communities. ⏱ 30 min. 207 Queens Quay W. ☎ 416/640-1571. www.miamuseum.ca. Admission $6 adults, $5 seniors and students, free for children 4 and under. Subway: Union (take either the 509 Exhibition or 510 Spadina streetcar west from inside Union Station and disembark on the third stop, Lower Simcoe St.).

⑩ Museum of Contemporary Canadian Art. Since it moved downtown to Queen West in 2005, the Museum of Contemporary Canadian Art has become more central to the local scene even as that scene itself moves farther away from the strip. A not-for-profit arm of the city's Cultural Services Section, it promotes innovative contemporary art and this mandate has led to exhibitions by such notables as Kent Monkman and Michael Snow, as well as group shows on such themes as street culture and food

The Museum of Inuit Art exhibits ancient and contemporary pieces.

The Museum of Canadian Contemporary Art exhibits and supports innovative Canadian art.

and art. ⏱ *30 min. 952 Queen St. W. ☎ 416/395-7598. www.mocca.ca. Admission PWYC. Tues–Sun 11am–6pm. Subway: Osgoode (from there, take the 501 streetcar west to Queen and Shaw).*

⑪ ★★ Katherine Mulherin Contemporary Art Projects.

The scene keeps moving in Toronto, from Queen West to West Queen West to Dundas and Ossington and beyond. But Katherine Mulherin, long considered the doyenne of Queen, remains in her popular space, continuing to spotlight many of the city's youngest, edgiest, and hippest artists, from the mischievous Seth Scriver to scenester Tyler Clark Burke. ⏱ *20 min. 1086 Queen St. W. ☎ 416/537-8827. www.katharinemulherin.com. Free admission. Thurs–Sun noon–5pm. Subway: Osgoode (from there, take the 501 streetcar west to Queen and Dovercourt).*

⑫ The Drake Hotel. Now a cultural landmark, this boutique hotel, open since 2004, is credited (or blamed) for transforming

West Queen West from a derelict neighborhood of vacant storefronts and artists' lofts into a vibrant, affluent strip of galleries, bars, and boutiques. (And subsequently, naturally, condos.) Purists grumble, but the hotel is also host to many exciting art events, from exhibits of Magnum photography to various Nuit Blanche spectacles. The Drake's permanent art collection, on display throughout the hotel's many publicly accessible levels, contains work by many emerging and established local artists. ⏱ *15 min. 1150 Queen St. W. ☎ 416/531-5042. www.thedrakehotel.ca. Subway: Osgoode (from there, take the 501 streetcar west to Queen and Beaconsfield).*

⑬ The Beaver Café. A great place to wrap up your tour, this gay-friendly hangout (co-owned by famed DJ and artist Will Munro) is the local for many artists, musicians, and fashionistas, Cheap and cheerful, it's good for sandwiches or late-night drinks. *1192 Queen St. W. ☎ 416/537-2768. $.*

Architectural Toronto

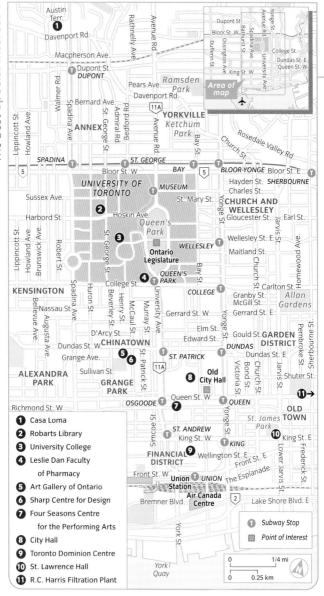

Area of map

1 Casa Loma
2 Robarts Library
3 University College
4 Leslie Dan Faculty
   of Pharmacy
5 Art Gallery of Ontario
6 Sharp Centre for Design
7 Four Seasons Centre
   for the Performing Arts
8 City Hall
9 Toronto Dominion Centre
10 St. Lawrence Hall
11 R.C. Harris Filtration Plant

🔵 Subway Stop
🔲 Point of Interest

0   1/4 mi
0   0.25 km

Downtown Toronto's architecture—an eclectic blend of Victorian, Edwardian, and brutalist buildings, for the most part—often gets a bad rap. But a closer look, preferably by foot, reveals abundant charm, eccentricity, and significance. This tour highlights several of the city's renowned and unusual buildings, many designed by some of the world's most famous architects and almost all within the downtown core. **START: Dupont Station.**

① Casa Loma. This is often dubbed "the city's most famous castle," but it could just as easily be called "the city's most famous folly." The former home of Sir Henry Pellatt, an industrialist fascinated by European castles, the building was designed in 1911 by architect E. J. Lennox in precisely those architectural terms. It boasts Elizabethan-style chimneys and Rhineland turrets, a 244m (800-ft.) underground tunnel and an 1,800-bottle wine cellar. The total cost of construction was $3.5 million and Pellatt only had 3 years to enjoy his precious home before financial misfortune forced him to abandon it. The gardens are a particular delight and open from May to October. ⏱ *2 hr. 1 Austin Terrace.* ☎ *416/923-1171. www.casaloma.org. Admission $18 adults, $13 seniors 60 and over and youth 14–17, $11 children 4–13. Subway: Dupont.*

② Robarts Library. The John P. Robarts Library at the University of Toronto is massive and also, to most eyes, massively ugly. The university's main humanities and social sciences library, it houses about five million books. It's a fine example of the city's brutalist tradition and many rumors swirl around the building: that it was designed to look like a peacock, that it's sinking a few centimeters every year because of the weight of the books, that it can withstand a nuclear blast. All apparently false. The adjoining Thomas Fisher Rare Book Library has a much more attractive interior and is also accessible to the public. ⏱ *30 min. 130 St. George St.* ☎ *416/978-8450. Subway: St. George.*

③ ★ University College. Many of the University of Toronto's neo-Gothic buildings are lovely to look at. This central edifice is exemplary

Casa Loma was built in 1911 for the wealthy industrialist Sir Henry Pellatt.

The Leslie Dan Faculty of Pharmacy was designed by British architect Norman Foster.

and includes a secluded courtyard, a serene quad, and a unique blend of architectural styles. An 1890 fire caused significant damage, but new decorative features were added during the reconstruction, including the building's adorable gargoyles. ⏱ *15 min. 15 King's College Circle.* ☎ *416/978-2968. Subway: St. George.*

④ ★ Leslie Dan Faculty of Pharmacy. This stunning, futuristic building was part of the University of Toronto's rapid expansion a few years ago. Designed by British architect Norman Foster, its unique first-floor "pods" house a classroom and a student lounge. ⏱ *15 min. 144 College St.* ☎ *416/978-2889. Subway: College.*

⑤ ★★★ Art Gallery of Ontario. The long-moribund Art Gallery of Ontario received a major makeover in 2008, courtesy of native son Frank Gehry. The redesign doesn't have quite the jaw-dropping flash of a Bilbao, but is certainly a vast and compelling improvement. The most dramatic and obvious feature is the 183m (600-ft.) glass-and-wood facade on Dundas Street (modeled after the shape of an overturned

canoe), but inside you'll find equally captivating sculptural staircases and light-filled walkways. ⏱ *2 hr. See p 48,* ❶.

⑥ ★★ Sharp Centre for Design. This is one of the city's most eccentric—and controversial—contemporary buildings. Designed by the English architect Will Alsop (his first North American building), the structure allowed the Ontario College of Art and Design to dramatically expand without requiring much more street-level space. Since the building opened in 2004, it's won numerous awards, one of which described it as "courageous, bold and just a little insane." ⏱ *10 min. 100 McCaul St.* ☎ *416/977-6000. Subway: St. Patrick.*

⑦ ★★ Four Seasons Centre for the Performing Arts. Jack Diamond, one of Toronto's most-celebrated architects, designed this subtly glorious building, which opened in 2006 after years of anticipation. The first venue in Canada built specifically for opera and ballet, it boasts state-of-the-art acoustics and construction materials (two Italian craftsmen came out of retirement to complete the Venetian plaster on the balconies). Building tours are available most Saturdays at noon. ⏱ *1 hr. See p 25,* ❻.

⑧ City Hall. For better or worse, this is a major modernist landmark for the city. Designed by the Finnish architect Viljo Revell and opened in 1965, the space-age structure—sometimes referred to as "The Clamshell"—consists of the flying-saucer-shaped Council Chamber centered between twin curving towers. Self-guided tours of the interior are available; brochures can be picked up at the information desk or on the website. The old city hall, a Victorian Romanesque–style building, is across the street at Bay and

The modernist, space-age design of City Hall was completed in 1965.

Queen. ⏱ *1 hr. 100 Queen St. W.* ☎ *416/338-0338. www.toronto.ca/ accesstoronto/self_guided_tour.htm. Subway: Queen.*

⑨ Toronto Dominion Centre. A set of six towers designed by the legendary Mies Van der Rohe, this complex is a black, steel-and-glass testament to Toronto's banking power. The first tower, the 55-story Toronto Dominion Bank Tower, was the first completed and officially opened on Canada's 100th birthday in 1967. Van der Rohe designed the landscaped plaza and courtyards as a space for art and public events, a kind of respite for the office workers that toil above. The underground mall below, containing more than 75 stores and restaurants, was the first in the city. ⏱ *30 min. 66 Wellington St. W.* ☎ *416/869-1144. Subway: King.*

⑩ St. Lawrence Hall. Designed and built in 1850, this Palladian-style building was once the center of

The Van der Rohe–designed Toronto Dominion Centre opened on Canada's 100th birthday.

community life in the city. It has hosted hundreds of public events— from political rallies to grand balls— and even a few bygone celebrities: **Tom Thumb, P.T. Barnum,** and **Jenny Lind,** to name a few. The building was meticulously restored in 1967 and its three main rooms are now home to conferences, meetings, and weddings; the plush, luxurious Great Hall, lit by an enormous gas-lit chandelier, is particularly romantic. ⏱ *15 min. 157 King St. E.* ☎ *416/392-7130. Subway: King.*

⑪ R. C. Harris Filtration Plant. A bit far-flung from downtown, this unusual edifice—once called the Palace of Purification—is worth the streetcar trip. Daily, about 200 million gallons of Lake Ontario water are treated and cleaned in this handsome, Art Deco–style facility, built in the '30s into the hills at the edge of the beach. The hallways are lined with French and Italian marble, and the plant is often featured in movies (*Strange Brew,* for one) and TV shows. The lake views are sublime. ⏱ *30 min. 2701 Queen St. E. www.toronto.ca/water/supply/ supply_facilities/rcharris. Subway: Queen, then #501 streetcar east.*

The Best Special-Interest Tours

Winter **Toronto**

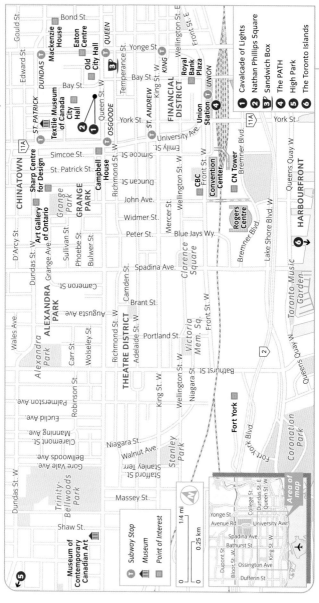

- ① Cavalcade of Lights
- ② Nathan Phillips Square
- ③ Sandwich Box
- ④ The PATH
- ⑤ High Park
- ⑥ The Toronto Islands

Legend:
- **T** Subway Stop
- 🏛 Museum
- ◼ Point of Interest

0 — 1/4 mi
0 — 0.25 km

Area of map

Toronto's not nearly as cold as many visitors expect, but this is still Canada, so if you're here between November and April, pack the mittens and prepare for a little bit of snow and ice. But don't worry, the city hardly stops. Far from it—some of its greatest pleasures can be had when the temperature drops.
START: **Queen Station.**

❶ ★ Cavalcade of Lights. Every year, from late November to the end of December, Toronto literally lights up. Twenty different neighborhoods—from Yorkville to Downsview—are draped with shimmering light displays, remarkable decorations, and gigantic Christmas trees. Chinatown is outfitted with dozens of illuminated lanterns and dragons, while City Hall and its surrounding buildings are gussied up with about 300,000 twinkling lights. A free 90-minute guided bus tour through several major neighborhoods runs from Thursday to Sunday, with pickup and drop-off at Nathan Phillips Square. *1½ hr. Free. Subway: Queen (walk west to Nathan Phillips Square, about 5 min.).*

❷ ★ Nathan Phillips Square. All winter long, the long reflecting pool in the shadow of City Hall is transformed into one of the city's most popular skating rinks. The rink's usually open from late November to the middle of March and

skates are available for rent. *1 hr. Subway: Queen (walk west to Nathan Phillips Square, about 5 min.).*

❸ ★ Sandwich Box. Fast-food maybe, but the unique, healthy soups, sandwiches, and salads at this boutique chain are made fresh daily. *67 Richmond St. W. (at Bay).* 📞 *416/913-4444. $.*

❹ The PATH. On those days when the temps do become Arctic, it's nice to know that there's a whole other city beneath the sidewalks. At 26km (16 miles) of interconnected, labyrinthine tunnels, packed with shops, offices, and restaurants, the PATH is the largest underground shopping complex in the world. Several tourist attractions—including the ACC and CN Tower—can also be entered through it. And it's linked at many locations to the subway system, so you can easily sample as much or as

Each winter, the city is magnificently decorated during the Cavalcade of Lights.

Santa Claus Is Coming to Town

Forget the temperature—winter doesn't really start in Toronto until the Santa Claus Parade (www.thesantaclausparade.ca) rolls into town. Every November since 1905, this extravagant parade (once bankrolled by Eaton's department store and now funded by a variety of corporate sponsors) brings together dozens of colorful floats, about 1,500 costumed volunteers, celebrity clowns, and, the coup de grâce, a jolly, candy-bestowing Saint Nick. About a half-million people, young and old, line the 5.7km (3.5-mile) route, which runs through the city from Bloor and Christie to Front and Church. Getting a sunny spot on a street like University Avenue, with its wide sidewalks, is ideal.

little as you like. First Canadian Place can be particularly compelling, with its fine array of shops and cultural events (even an art gallery). But do stay underground long enough to warm up! ⏱ *1 hr. Subway: Union.*

❺ ★★ kids High Park. Toronto's largest park is transformed into a winter wonderland once the snow starts to fly. The hiking trails are groomed and maintained for cross-country skiing, while winter wildlife walking tours and holiday hikes continue throughout the season. ⏱ *1 hr. See p 18,* ❶.

❻ ★★ kids The Toronto Islands. While it might seem counterintuitive to head to the Islands in winter, the colder months can be a truly magical time to visit. The sound of the ferry breaking through icy water is eerie and, buried beneath snow, the islanders' homes are transformed into a fairy-tale village. It's blustery, to be sure, and the usual attractions are closed, but you can count on having large parts of the park to yourself. A pair of snowshoes or cross-country skis comes in handy. ⏱ *2 hr. See p 94.* ●

Fans line the streets to see the guest of honor at the Santa Claus Parade.

Yorkville and the Mink Mile

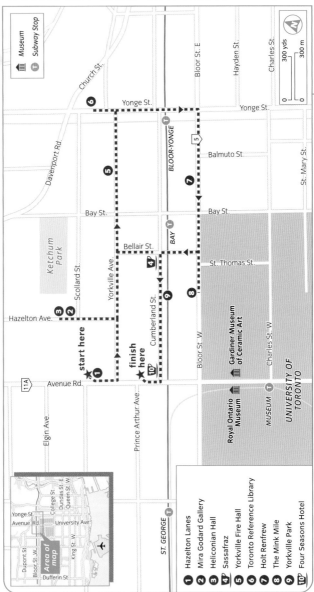

● Hazelton Lanes
● Mira Godard Gallery
● Heliconian Hall
● Sassafraz
● Yorkville Fire Hall
● Toronto Reference Library
● Holt Renfrew
● The Mink Mile
● Yorkville Park
● Four Seasons Hotel

Previous page: The Gooderham Flatiron building is one of the most photographed sites in town.

Yorkville was once its own small town—annexed by Toronto in 1883—and throughout its history, the neighborhood has retained a defiant, independent spirit. In the '60s, that spirit was bohemian (Joni Mitchell and Neil Young got their start here), but today, it's one of exclusiveness and wealth—this is where the city's elite come to be seen, shop, and dine. On summer nights, the purr of Lamborghinis can be deafening, but the narrow streets and cobblestone courtyards are perfect for casual strolls. START: **Bay Station.**

1 Hazelton Lanes. For more than 30 years, this 18,581sq. m (200,000-sq.-ft.) shopping mall has been an emblem of Yorkville's high-flying, luxurious retail ambition. But in recent years, as Bloor Street has claimed prize flagship boutiques like Gucci and Prada, Hazelton's halls can feel eerily quiet, with many of the storefronts empty. Its prime tenant, now, however, is Whole Foods and the upscale grocer is always brimming with brie-hunting condo dwellers. ⏲ *1 hr. 87 Avenue Rd.* ☎ *416/968-8680.*

2 ★★ Mira Godard Gallery. While the more adventurous galleries have moved farther downtown, Yorkville is still home to many blue-chip dealers. Mira Godard is one of the oldest commercial galleries in the country, established in 1962,

and its beautiful three floors of exhibition space feature such Canadian and international artists as Alex Colville, Andy Goldsworthy, and Christopher Pratt. ⏲ *30 min. 22 Hazelton Ave.* ☎ *416/964-8197. Free admission. Tues–Sat 10am–5pm.*

3 Heliconian Hall. Built in 1875, this quaint, former church now serves as the headquarters for the Toronto Heliconian Club, a social club for women in the arts and letters. The original board and batten structure has been preserved and renovated and designated a national historic site in 2008. Now rented out for performances and events, several notables have graced its halls, from John Gielgud to writer Mavis Gallant. ⏲ *15 min. 35 Hazelton Ave.* ☎ *416/922-3618.*

Hazelton Lanes has been an emblem of Yorkville for more than 30 years.

Mira Godard is one of the oldest commercial art galleries in the country.

4 Sassafraz. Smack-dab in the middle of Yorkville, this corner bistro—a large, inviting yellow house—is known more for being a prime people-watching perch than for its food. A 2006 fire gutted the restaurant but its rapid rebuilding speaks to the place it enjoys in the neighborhood's heart. Sample one of 7,000 wines on the sidewalk patio or the new rooftop patio. *100 Cumberland St.* ☎ *416/964-2222. $$.*

5 Yorkville Fire Hall. This charming fire station was built in 1876 and restored in 1974. The coat of arms from the old Yorkville Town Hall, destroyed by fire, coincidentally, in 1941, hangs here above the main door. *34 Yorkville Ave.*

6 ★ Toronto Reference Library. Toronto has the largest public library system in Canada and one of the busiest in the world. This, its flagship branch, is a spectacular late '70s glass-and-brick edifice, its interior atrium flooded with light. Ajon Moriyama, son of Raymond Moriyama, the original architect, is responsible for a multimillion-dollar renovation that began in 2009. ⏱ *15 min. 789 Yonge St.* ☎ *416/ 395-5577.*

7 ★★ Holt Renfrew. The chicest (if snootiest) department store in town is five floors of top-line designer clothing and accessories. Established in 1837, Holt has its roots in the Quebec fur trade, and while fur is still a staple, customers

Stargazers

Celeb spotting during September's Toronto International Film Festival is a bit of a sport for many Torontonians. But there are better ways to see Brangelina than joining the amateur papparazi lurking around the Four Seasons Hotel. For one, go inside the hotel. You can easily park yourself in the Lobby Bar and enjoy high tea (p 57) while watching the stars come and go. Other choice spots: poolside at the Intercontinental Toronto Yorkville Hotel (p 148), the patio at One (p 111), and the Park Hyatt Roof Lounge (p 123).

are more likely to come for the Marc Jacobs and Etro. Expensive, to be sure, but frequent "designer sales" knock prices down as much as 60%. If you have no time to shop, the witty window displays on Bloor are always worth a look. ⏱ *1 hr. 50 Bloor St. W.* ☎ *416/922-2333.*

❽ The Mink Mile. Long described as Toronto's answer to Rodeo Drive or Fifth Avenue, this swanky stretch of Bloor, from Avenue to Yonge, is home to dozens of upscale shops, from high-end menswear department store, Harry Rosen, to Chanel and Tiffany. The Collonade and Manulife Centre, both shopping areas–cum–apartment towers, are examples of the brutalist architecture that swept the city in the '60s and '70s. A beautification of the strip, begun in 2008, widened sidewalks and increased the public art and number of trees (though cycling activists have bemoaned the lack of bike lanes).

❾ ★★ Yorkville Park. The enormous granite boulder at the edge of this urban oasis is roughly 650 tons of billion-year-old Canadian Shield rock. It is a renowned meeting spot and a

The 650-ton rock in Yorkville Park is an excellent meeting place.

superb vantage spot for film-festival celebrity spotting. *See p 9,* ❶.

➓ ★★ Four Seasons Hotel. Wrap up your tour with a relaxing, late-afternoon tea. The luxe hotel's version, held in its bright Lobby Bar, is classic and sumptuous. The menu typically includes cucumber and watercress sandwiches, scones and tortes, and an extensive range of tea blends. *21 Avenue Rd.* ☎ *416/964-0411. Afternoon tea Mon–Fri 2:30–5:30pm, Sat–Sun 1:30–5:30pm. $$.*

Chic Holt Renfrew often features designer sales.

Queen Street West

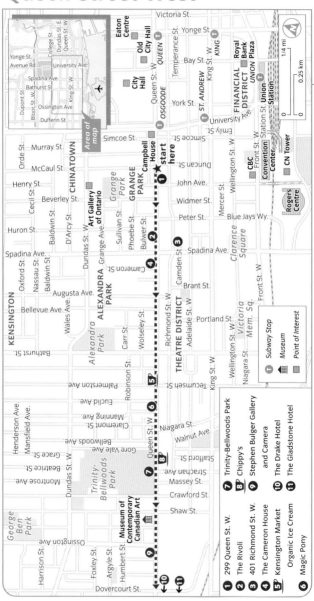

1/4 mi
0.25 km

Area of map

Subway Stop
Museum
Point of Interest

1 299 Queen St. W.
2 The Rivoli
3 401 Richmond St. W.
4 The Cameron House
5 Kensington Market
Organic Ice Cream
6 Magic Pony
7 Trinity-Bellwoods Park
8 Chippy's
9 Stephen Bulger Gallery and Camera
10 The Drake Hotel
11 The Gladstone Hotel

owntown's accelerated gentrification has pushed Queen West's traditional bohemian enclave so far westward that half of this long strip, from Bathurst to Dufferin, is now called West Queen West (or, depending on who you ask, Queen West West or the Art and Design District). Following the money trail today, you can actually trace this spirited commercial and artistic evolution, while still taking in many cultural landmarks. START: **St. Patrick Station.**

❶ 299 Queen St. W. Formerly the MuchMusic/CityTV Building, this handsome neo-Gothic building is now the main studio for new owners, the Canadian Television Network (CTV), and its flagship entertainment program, *eTalk Daily*. An old CityTV news truck that appears to have flown into the side of the building remains. As Much-Music and City TV did, CTV continues to host many events inside and outside the building—especially during the film festival—that attract hordes of adoring fans. ⏱ *1 hr.*

❷ The Rivoli. One of the Queen West's first hot spots in the early '80s, "the Riv" remains both landmark and throwback. The Kids in the Hall got their start in the back room and I've attended a diverse range of events here, from a Cowboy Junkies concert to a lecture by filmmaker Atom Egoyan. The food is still decent (try the satay), comedy is

401 Richmond St. W. houses some of the city's hippest galleries and arts groups.

still a staple, and the crowd is still a diverse blend of musicians, artists, and actors. ⏱ *30 min. 334 Queen St. W.* ☎ *416/596-1908.*

299 Queen St. W. hosts many events inside and outside the building.

Trinity-Bellwoods Park is popular on summer days.

❸ ★★★ 401 Richmond St. W.
It's well worth taking a slight tour south to check out this wonderful building, a former lithography factory that now houses some of the city's hippest galleries and most dynamic arts groups. Owned by the Zeidler family (see "The Zeidler Effect," p 25), it's a vibrant, mixed-use, five-story structure whose sunny spaces and studios are home to artists like John Scott; the über-cool design bookshop, Swipe; and innovative photography gallery, Pre-fix. Delightful green roofs and vertical gardens contribute to the utopian character of the place. ⏲ *2 hr. Group tours can be arranged by calling* ☎ *416/595-5900.*

❹ The Cameron House. The Cameron recently celebrated 25 years of bringing edgy theater and cheap drinks to the Queen West masses. A working hotel and bar for about 80 years, since 1981 the watering hole's small stages have hosted all kinds of artists and scenesters, most famously Video-Cabaret, the political theater troupe, and the alternative-lecture series, Trampoline Hall. If you're lucky, the chatty Andy Patterson will bring you your beer—he's an artist and Queen Street fixture who also lives upstairs. ⏲ *1 hr. 408 Queen St. W.* ☎ *416/703-0811.*

❺ ★★ Kensington Market Organic Ice Cream. Don't let the name fool you—this mercurial artisanal ice cream maker is just around the corner. It's a tiny shop but there are more than 30 flavors available; make sure you try the distinctly Canadian chestnut-and-birch syrup blend. *650½ Queen St. W.* ☎ *416/801-4970. $.*

❻ ★ kids Magic Pony. Some contend that Toronto's art scene tends too much to the twee and this whimsical shop-cum-gallery is definitely evidence of that—much of the merchandise is just too cute for words. While initially specializing in art, toys, and stuffed animals from Asia, Magic Pony expanded to include cutting-edge work from Canadian and international artists like Gary Taxali, Sonja Ahlers, and Derrick Hodgson. Regular events are held in the gallery and a new exhibition space at 680 Queen St. W. ⏲ *30 min. 694 Queen St. W.* ☎ *416/861-1684.*

7 ★★ **kids Trinity-Bellwoods Park.** Not too long ago this was a desolate bit of greenery, a no man's land frequented mainly by prostitutes and dog walkers. Today, it's a charming spot where, on summer days, the tennis courts and baseball diamonds are full, hipsters are playing croquet, and kids are frolicking on the jungle gyms. Once the site of Trinity College (now part of the University of Toronto), the stone and wrought-iron gates at Queen and Strachan are all that remain, and the large bowl in the middle of the park is the original Garrison Creek ravine (the creek itself is buried). Dog owners still love it. ⏲ *1 hr. Queen St. W. at Gore Vale Ave.*

8 **Chippy's.** If you can stand the musical assault that greets you when you walk into this tiny fish-and-chips shop, you'll walk out with a great, greasy picnic lunch. The fish comes in a Guinness beer batter and the fresh-cut fries are wonderful dipped in hot curry gravy. *893 Queen St. W.* ☎ *416/866-7474. $.*

9 ★ **The Stephen Bulger Gallery and Camera.** The Stephen Bulger Gallery is the city's preeminent photography gallery (representing Robert Burley, Mary Ellen Mark, and others) and Camera is an elegant 50-seat screening lounge/bar that's co-owned by filmmaker Atom Egoyan. While the latter's regular programming has largely stopped (it's used now for private screenings and parties, although the bar is still a nice place for a drink), the two spaces are often combined for large exhibition events. ⏲ *30 min. 1026 Queen St. W.* ☎ *416/504-0575.*

10 ★★ **The Drake Hotel.** This boutique hotel was ground zero for the transformation of West Queen West from a sleepy, derelict strip of appliance stores to a playground for the beautiful people. Torontonians thus love it and hate it in equal measure, but it's still a great place for exceptional food and entertainment. ⏲ *1 hr. See p 45,* **12**.

11 ★★★ **The Gladstone Hotel.** Renovated and reopened not too long after the Drake, the Gladstone's kind of the Chelsea to the former's Bowery Hotel. The Gladstone tends to attract less-flashy, more-compelling entertainment and a lot more locals. ⏲ *1 hr. See p 27,* **10**.

The Gladstone Hotel features artist-designed rooms and compelling entertainment.

Chinatown & Kensington Market

1. Dragon City
2. Oriental Harvest
3. Forestview
4. Tap Phong
5. Bungalow
6. Bellevue Square Park
7. Kiever Synagogue
8. Hot Box Café
9. Cheese Magic
10. Courage My Love

Stroll up Spadina Avenue—one of the city's broadest bou-levards—and you'll be treated to a tantalizing array of cultures, foods, sights, and smells. This strip is one of the most storied in Toronto, and speaks like no other to the compelling, multicultural development of the city. And moving from Chinatown to the Market is as close to international travel—even time travel—as you can get by moving a block's radius. START: **Spadina and Dundas.**

❶ Dragon City. For a taste of Hong Kong, step into this three-story shopping complex, situated right in the heart of Chinatown. More than 30 stores carry everything from herbal remedies to Asian music CDs. Rooftop restaurant Sky Dragon isn't the best in the hood, but the view is nice. 🕐 *1 hr. 280 Spadina Ave.*

❷ ★ Oriental Harvest. Crowded, yes, but cheap, clean, and crammed with all manner of Chinese preserves, fresh fish (there are tanks full of live snappers and crabs), and dozens of exotic veggies and fruit. A whole aisle

of this market is devoted to different kinds of noodles. The signage is good, in English and Chinese. 🕐 *30 min. 310 Spadina Ave.* ☎ *416/581-8666.*

❸ ★ Forestview. Fortifying dim sum is served up at this busy, if basic, second-floor restaurant from 11am to 4pm. Servers are especially friendly and the classics—beef meatballs, shrimp cheong fan, deep-fried bean-curd wraps—are well turned out and well priced. *466 Dundas St. W. (at Spadina)* ☎ *416/597-0319. $$.*

Dragon City is a three-story shopping complex in the heart of Chinatown.

The Best Neighborhood Walks

Tap Phong is beloved for its array of Asian knick-knacks.

④ ★★ Tap Phong. This Chinatown institution—a fave with beloved local politician Olivia Chow—carries everything you need to outfit your own restaurant or first apartment. Grab one of the cheap plastic tubs outside (which start at $1.50) and fill it up with as much Buddhist statuary, cutlery, baskets, tea sets, and electronic devices you can manage. Brands range from the biggest to the most basic, as well as many legible only to Mandarin readers. ⏱ *30 min. 360 Spadina Ave.* ☎ *416/977-6364.*

⑤ ★ Bungalow. A harbinger of Kensington's latest wave of gentrification, this 279sq.-m (3,000-sq.-ft.) shop carries everything from well-priced vintage clothing to midcentury modern furniture and housewares. There's new clothing, as well, from Obey and B. B. Dakota, and Bungalow's signature "remade" fashions—one-of-a-kind shirts, silk-screened suit jackets, and reworked cashmere sweaters. ⏱ *15 min. 273 Augusta Ave.* ☎ *416/598-0204.*

⑥ ★★ kids Bellevue Square Park. Kensington's more colorful denizens take over this parkette in summer and you'll see punks playing with their dogs, aging hippies tossing a Frisbee around, and hipsters holding hands. Kids can cool off in the wading pool or clamber over the monkey bars. In the northwest corner of the park is a statue of actor Al Waxman, most famous for playing the king of Kensington in the long-running CBC TV series of the same name. ⏱ *15 min.*

⑦ ★ Kiever Synagogue. A reminder of when the Market was known as the "Jewish Market," this shul, first opened in 1917 (with construction completed in 1927), was the first specifically Jewish landmark designated a historic site by the province of Ontario. The synagogue was designed by architect Benjamin Swartz, blending Romanesque and

Walk This Way

On the last Sunday of every month from May to October, Kensington Market is closed to cars and the narrow streets, which are best for walking anyway, become home to a lively, family-friendly carnival. The brainchild of Shamez Amlani, owner of the restaurant La Palette, Pedestrian Sundays (www.pskensington.ca) brings out a diverse range of free entertainment—buskers, yoga demos, stilt walkers—as well as tasty street food, fashion shows, and lots of impromptu dancing. The fest has been so successful, it's expanded to other avenues—Baldwin Street on the other side of Chinatown and Mirvish Village in the Annex.

Cheese Magic specializes in artisanal cheeses from Quebec.

Byzantine styles, its twin, domed towers crowned by the Star of David. ⏱ *15 min. 25 Bellevue Ave.* ☎ *416/593-9702.*

❽ Hot Box Café. While marijuana is still technically illegal in Canada, its use is more tolerated here than in many other countries. So much so, in fact, that this discreet cafe at the back of the Roach-O-Rama store is the first pot-positive cafe in the country. Of course, you can't buy drugs on the premises, but anyone who is so inclined can bring their own and smoke it in peace. Or just enjoy the contact high as you nibble on a Ganja Lovers Grilled Cheese or Hemp Nut Caesar Salad. (The bad puns don't stop there—the patio's called the "potio.") Maximum stay is 1 hour and there's a $2 minimum. ⏱ *30 min. 191A Baldwin Ave.* ☎ *416/203-6990.*

❾ ★ Cheese Magic. Kensington Market isn't the *best* place to get cheese in the city, but it's one of the cheapest. This tiny shop, staffed by young men famed for their broody good looks, serves up a nice range of cheeses from around the world. Artisanal Quebec cheeses are a specialty, as well as organic raw-milk cheddar. The small olive bar and a good selection of crackers and

breads are bonuses. ⏱ *15 min. 182 Baldwin St.* ☎ *416/593-9531.*

❿ ★★ kids Courage My Love. The Market has long been a mecca for lovers of vintage clothing. Courage My Love is the best of the bunch. The long, narrow shop, open since 1975, is packed to the rafters with retro gowns, suits, and quirky accessories. Teens love the dizzying selection of beads and the shop owners make frequent trips abroad, bringing back a wide range of colorful jewelry and fabrics. ⏱ *30 min. 14 Kensington Ave.* ☎ *416/979-1992.*

Nibble on Ganja Lovers Grilled Cheese or Hemp Nut Caesar Salad at the Hot Box Café.

Church Street & Cabbagetown

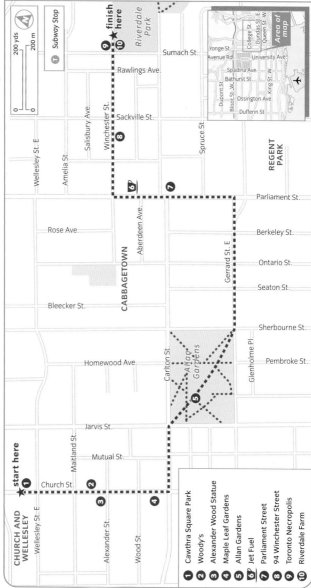

- ❶ Cawthra Square Park
- ❷ Woody's
- ❸ Alexander Wood Statue
- ❹ Maple Leaf Gardens
- ❺ Allan Gardens
- ❻ Jet Fuel
- ❼ Parliament Street
- ❽ 94 Winchester Street
- ❾ Toronto Necropolis
- ❿ Riverdale Farm

start here ❶

finish here ❾ ❿

CHURCH AND WELLESLEY

CABBAGETOWN

REGENT PARK

Allan Gardens

Riverdale Park

Area of map

🚇 Subway Stop

200 yds

200 m

Alternately drab and delightful, Church and Wellesley is the heart of the city's gay and lesbian community (hence the affectionate nicknames, the Gay Village, Boystown, and the Gayborhood). Nearby Cabbagetown was once a slum full of the Irish immigrants who arrived in the 1840s and now encompasses both one of the city's most exclusive enclaves and its grittiest low-income housing. START: **Wellesley Station.**

① ★★ Cawthra Square Park. Located behind the 519 Community Centre, this parkette is home to the Toronto AIDS Memorial, a set of concrete pillars upon which are affixed stainless steel plaques emblazoned with the names of those lost to the disease. A candlelight vigil is held here during the Gay Pride festivities every June. *519 Church St.*

② Woody's. If any bar can be said to epitomize the strip's nightlife, this cavernous institution is it. Now 20 years old, the club (and the adjoining watering hole, Sailor) is actually five bars in one, notorious for its nightly contests (Best Chest, and so forth) and its large windows—in summer, these are wide open, allowing a great view of the busy street below. *467 Church St.* ☎ *416/972-0887.*

③ ★ Alexander Wood Statue. The 2.4m (8-ft.) bronze statue at the corner of Church and Alexander streets honors a Scottish merchant and gay pioneer who immigrated to Toronto in 1797. Aside from a Georgian silhouette portrait, no other images of Wood exist; sculptor Del Newbigging worked from the silhouette and clothing research, adding what he called "gay flair." It's thought to be the only monument of its kind in the world. *Corner of Church and Alexander Sts.*

④ Maple Leaf Gardens. The legendary, much-cherished home of the Toronto Maple Leafs hockey team from 1931 to 1999, this arena has sat empty ever since the Leafs left. (The Leafs now play at the Air Canada Centre.) The country's largest grocery store chain, Loblaw, bought the complex in 2004 and various redevelopment schemes have been floated ever since, so far amounting to nothing. There's been some welcome activity in the last couple of years, however, with the venue being used for events during the **Toronto International Film Festival** and **Nuit Blanche.** *60 Carlton St. (at Church).*

⑤ ★★ Allan Gardens. Toronto's very first civic park, this green space's proximity to a famed prostitutes' stroll and various seedy quarters left it derelict and dangerous. These days, thanks to an earnest revitalization plan, it's once again a kind of oasis, with its six greenhouses a popular tourist attraction

Alexander Wood was an 18th-century gay pioneer.

The revitalized Allan Gardens features six greenhouses open to the public.

(particularly the Palm House, built in 1910) and a new off-leash area popular with local dog owners. *Carlton and Sherbourne.* ☎ *416/392-7288. Greenhouses open daily 10am–5pm. Free admission.*

❻ Jet Fuel. There's nothing less like Starbucks than this landmark coffee shop, notorious for its lack of menu, lack of food, and lots of attitude. But the lattes are lovely and, if you're a cyclist, you'll appreciate the cafe's longstanding support of couriers (they even sponsor a bike team). *519 Parliament St.* ☎ *416/968-9982. $.*

❼ Parliament Street. The neighborhood's main drag has never been quite as swanky as the price of the neighborhood's charming Victorians would suggest. Lower-income neighborhoods like St. Jamestown and Regent Park, currently undergoing a massive revitalization, bracket the strip, but in between you can find a pleasant array of restaurants and bars (recommended: the Cobourg and the House on Parliament), antiques stores, and food shops. The name of the street comes from the fact that the first Upper Canada government buildings were built at its foot between 1794 and 1797.

Cabbagetown Charm

It's often said that the leafy, narrow streets of Cabbagetown contain the largest continuous area of Victorian housing in North America. The Cabbagetown Preservation Association was founded in 1988 to preserve the architectural integrity of these beautiful and unique homes and much of the area was designated a Heritage Conservation District in 2001. Some notable streets to stroll down include Winchester, Parkview, and the alleys of Woodstock Place and Wellesley Street East.

8 94 Winchester Street. Many famous Torontonians have lived in Cabbagetown, from poet Al Purdy to architect Eden Smith. None may be more famous, however, than Doug Henning, magician, teacher, and politician (he ran, unsuccessfully, as a candidate for the fringe Natural Law Party). The late prestidigitator, who died in 2000, lived on the third floor of this house in 1969, when he first embarked on his study of magic. You can't go inside, but a plaque outside explains all. *A block and a half east of Parliament.*

9 ★★★ Toronto Necropolis. So beautiful and yet still so spooky, this is the city's most beguiling cemetery. Its inhabitants aren't necessarily the most famous (those would be up in Mount Pleasant) but there are some well-known graves, including those of George Brown, a journalist who founded the *Globe and Mail* newspaper, and William Lyon Mackenzie, the city's first mayor. Some of Toronto's finest High Victorian Gothic architecture is to be found here—the cemetery was established in 1850—especially the large archway that you first walk

Cabbagetown is home to the largest continuous area of Victorian housing in North America.

through. Free maps can be picked up at the entrance. *200 Winchester St.* ☎ *416/923-7911.*

10 ★★ kids Riverdale Farm. After you visit the animals, wander over for a rest in the adjoining park. If it's a summer Tuesday between 3 and 7pm, the farmers' market should be in full swing. *See p 37,* **5**.

Kids love visiting the animals at Riverdale Farm.

St. Lawrence Market &
the Distillery District

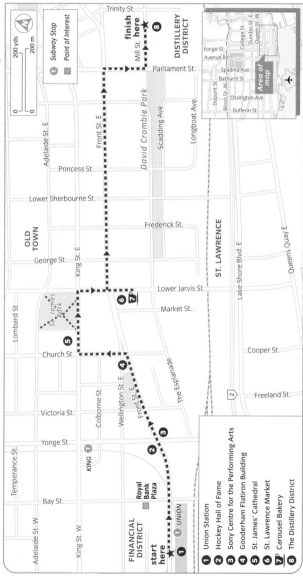

Trinity St.

finish
here

DISTILLERY
DISTRICT

Mill St.

Parliament St.

Yonge St.
Avenue Rd

Spadina Ave.

Bathurst St.

Dupont St.
Bloor St. W.

Ossington Ave.

Dufferin St.

College St.
Dundas St. E
Queen St. W

Area of
map

Front St. E

Adelaide St. E

David Crombie Park

Scadding Ave.

Longboat Ave.

Princess St.

Lower Sherbourne St.

OLD
TOWN

Frederick St.

George St.

King St. E

ST. LAWRENCE

Lower Jarvis St.

Market St.

Lombard St.

St. James
Park

Church St.

Lake Shore Blvd. E

Queens Quay E

Cooper St.

Victoria St.

Colborne St.

Wellington St. E

Front St.

The Esplanade

Freeland St.

Yonge St.

KING

Temperance St.

Royal
Bank
Plaza

FINANCIAL
DISTRICT

start
here

UNION

Bay St.

Adelaide St. W

King St. W

200 yds
200 m

Subway Stop
Point of Interest

1 Union Station
2 Hockey Hall of Fame
3 Sony Centre for the Performing Arts
4 Gooderham Flatiron Building
5 St. James' Cathedral
6 St. Lawrence Market
7 Carousel Bakery
8 The Distillery District

In this lengthy tour, you'll traverse what's now prosaically known as Old Town and end up in one of the city's newest neighborhoods, the much-ballyhooed Distillery District. Along the way, you'll be in the presence of some of Toronto's oldest, and most stunning, architecture. Don't forget to look up. (And bring your wallet; there's some good shopping at the end.) START: **Union Station.**

① ★ Union Station. In 1927, the Prince of Wales opened this immense railroad station with the words, "You build your stations like we build our cathedrals." The 250,000-odd passengers that flow through every day may not have such poetic thoughts as they bump up against their fellow commuters, but visitors should definitely pause and take in the station's grandeur and Beaux Arts design. (An exclusive, almost secret, shooting range in the building was used by police and others until it was shut down in 2008.) There was much buzz about Union's overhaul (including new passageways and retail) but progress has been plodding. Transit buffs can take a free 45-minute tour of the station during Doors Open in May (see "Doors Open," below). ⏱ *30 min. 65 Front St. W.*

② ★★ Hockey Hall of Fame. In 1885, this remarkable rococo building was the head office of the Bank of Montreal—one of the few structures to survive Toronto's Great Fire of 1904. Just over 100 years later, this temple of commerce became a temple dedicated to Canada's most-beloved sport. More than half a million fans visited in its first year of operation. Home to the Stanley Cup, the complex also houses hundreds of artifacts, uniforms, memorabilia, skills-testing interactive games, and a replica of the legendary Montreal Canadiens dressing room. ⏱ *2 hr. Brookfield Place, 30 Yonge St.* ☎ *416/360-7735. www.hhof.com. Admission $13 adults, $9 seniors 65 and over and youth 4–13, free for children 3 and under. Summer Mon–Sat 9:30am–6pm, Sun 10am–6pm; winter, spring, and fall, Mon–Fri 10am–5pm, Sat 9:30am–6pm, Sun 10:30am–5pm.*

③ Sony Centre for the Performing Arts. The building, formerly known as the O'Keefe Centre and the Hummingbird Centre, was

The Hockey Hall of Fame is home to the Stanley Cup and a replica of the legendary Montreal Canadiens dressing room.

The Distillery District has been transformed from an abandoned manufacturing area to an inviting entertainment region.

built in 1960 (Baryshnikov defected here) and, until the opening of the Four Seasons Centre (p 25), was home to the National Ballet and Canadian Opera Company. With those two major companies gone, programming became more diverse and multicultural—the centre's shown theatrical work from Korea, South Asia, and the Ukraine. In 2008, a massive $75-million renovation began, with ROM Crystal mastermind Daniel Libeskind at the helm. *1 Front St. E. ☎ 416/872-2262. www.sonycentre.ca.*

④ ★ Gooderham Flatiron Building. Still one of the most-photographed sights in town, the five-story Flatiron, situated on a tiny wedge of land at the intersection of Wellington and Front, was the head office of the Gooderham and Worts Distillery until 1952. While there are now flatiron-style buildings around the world, Toronto's Gothic Romanesque version was reportedly the first. Today, its office space is some of the city's most expensive and tenants include law firms and the popular Flatiron & Firkin pub in the basement. Don't forget to check out the *trompe l'oeil* mural on the back of the building.

⑤ St. James' Cathedral. This majestic Anglican cathedral began life as the first wooden Church of York in 1807, before a neoclassical-style renovation in 1833. (The town of York became the City of Toronto in 1834.) That church was destroyed

Doors Open

In 2000, Toronto initiated the very first North American Doors Open event, designed to open up to the general public many of the city's most treasured private and government buildings, homes, and architectural marvels. Now held every May, Doors Open (www.doorsopenontario.on.ca) has grown incredibly (more than 150 buildings participate) and the free tours now include everything from the Distillery's underground tunnels to the inner chambers of the CBC Broadcast Centre.

by fire in 1849 and the Gothic revival cathedral that stands today replaced it in 1853. It's since been expanded and renovated frequently, with a major renovation completed in 1982. The bell tower (one of the tallest in the world, at 93m/305 ft.) houses the Bells of Old York, 12 change-ringing bells that provide the only ring of its kind in North America.

⑥ St. Lawrence Market. *Food & Wine* magazine named this one of the world's best farmers' markets and although the actual farmers' market is only open on Saturday (in the north building), the south market serves as a foodie paradise the rest of the week. It's packed on weekends, but, aside from the long lines from the lunchtime hordes, weekdays are surprisingly crowd free. While there are dozens of permanent vendors, selling everything from horse meat to horseradish, be sure to make stops at Aton Kozlik's Canadian Mustard and Chris's Cheesemongers, specializing in artisanal Canadian and Italian fromage. ⏱ *1 hr. 92 Front St. E.*

St. Lawrence Market is a foodie paradise.

⑦ Carousel Bakery. There are a few stalls in the Market selling peameal bacon sandwiches but this 30-year-old institution makes the yummiest. Don't let the line scare you off. *St. Lawrence Market, 93 Front St. E.* ☎ *416/863-6764. $.*

⑧ The Distillery District. This whimsical warren of converted Victorian buildings has become, with the

Toronto's flatiron-style building is reportedly the world's oldest example of the style.

growth of the condos above and beside it, like a little village unto itself. Almost everything you want is here—good food and drink, brilliant art, high-end shopping, and fine

entertainment. Appropriately, it's also the site of several of the city's best cultural festivals, from the Art of Jazz fest in June to Nuit Blanche in the fall.

Distillery District

Front St. E

Parliament St.

Trinity St.

Cherry St.

Mill St.

8A **8F**

8E

P

8B **8C 8D** P

**DISTILLERY
DISTRICT**

Gardiner Expressway

Lake Shore Blvd. E

2

0   50 yds
0   50 m

P *Parking*

Just inside the main gate of the Distillery is the **8A** **Brick Street Bakery** (☎ 416/214-4925), which specializes in organic British-style breads and pastries. At the end of this cobble-stone boulevard, Trinity Street, you'll see (in the main square) an 11-meter-tall (36 foot) aluminum and steel sculpture called **8B** *Still Dancing,* by renowned conceptualist Dennis Oppenheim. More art—and crafts—awaits next door, in the **8C** **Case Goods Warehouse,** where dozens of artisans and craftspeople maintain studios and small boutiques. **8D** **Akroyd Furniture** (☎ 416/367-5757) makes works of particular beauty, handcrafted

furniture hewn from local wood. Heading into the heart of the district, you could stop for some restorative seafood at **8E** **Pure Spirits Oyster House and Grill** (☎ 416/361-5859) or simply marvel at the transformation of a 130-year-old barrel shipping room into a cozy, high-end eatery. A bit further along is the crown jewel of the complex, the **8F** **Young Centre for the Performing Arts** (☎ 416/866-8666). Formerly a set of tank houses, the unique 50,000-square-foot building is both educational facility and prized theatrical venue, home to the renowned Soulpepper Theatre Company. *See p 15,* **7**. ●

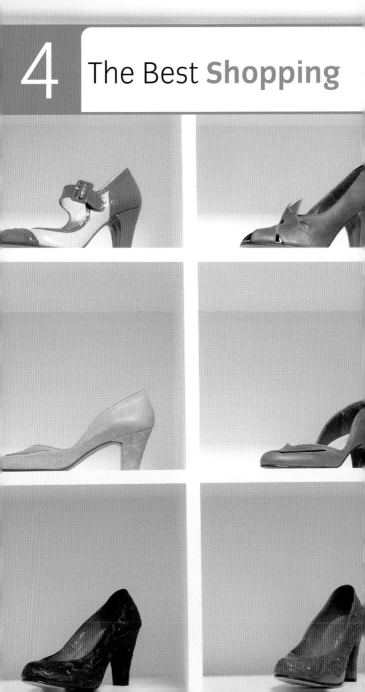

Shopping Best Bets

Ella and Elliott appeals to kids of all ages.

Best **Perfumery**
★★★ Noor, *176 Cumberland St.*
(p 82)

Best **Bespoke Men's Jeans**
★★★ Sydney's, *795 Queen St. W.*
(p 85)

Best **Vintage**
★ 69 Vintage, *1100 Queen St. W.*
(p 88)

Best **Shop for Chefs**
★★ Good Egg, *267 Augusta Ave.*
(p 81)

Most **Unique Gifts**
★★ Studio Brillantine, *1518 Queen St. W. (p 86)*

Best **Cozy Bookshop**
★★★ Type, *883 Queen St. W. (p 81)*

Best **Clothing Boutique for Friendly Service**
★ Jonathan and Olivia, *49 Ossington Ave. (p 84)*

Best **Off-Beat Canadian Furniture**
★★ MADE, *867 Dundas St. W. (p 85)*

Best **Locally Made Handbags**
★ Virginia Johnson, *132 Ossington Ave. (p 85)*

Best **Shop to Bump into Budding Indie Rockers**
★★★ Soundscapes, *572 College St. (p 87)*

Best **High-End Toys**
★★ Ella and Elliot, *188 Strachan Ave. (p 88)*

Best **One-Stop Fashion**
★ Holt Renfrew, *50 Bloor St. W. (p 83)*

Best **Shop for Design Geeks**
★★ Swipe, *401 Richmond St. W. (p 81)*

Best **Place for Surreal Shoe Designs**
John Fluevog, *242 Queen St. W. (p 88)*

Best **Place for Affordable Antiques**
GUFF, *1152 Queen St. E. (p 82)*

Best **Place for Eccentric Used Books**
★★ The Monkey's Paw, *1229 Dundas St. W. (p 81)*

Best **Mall for Kids**
Eaton Centre, *220 Yonge St. (p 87)*

Previous page: Women's shoes from Trove.

Midtown Shopping

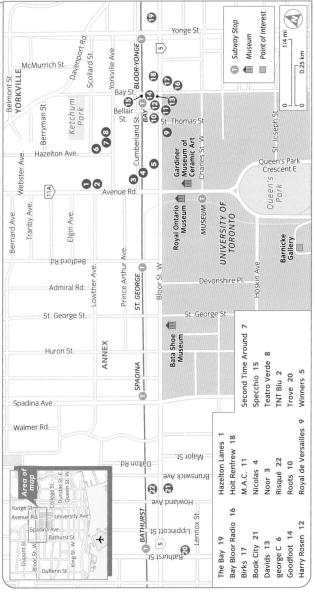

Legend

- T — Subway Stop
- 🏛 — Museum
- ⬛ — Point of Interest

0   0.25 km
0   1/4 mi

Yonge St.
McMurrich St.
Belmont St.
YORKVILLE
Davenport Rd.
Scollard St.
Yorkville Ave.
BLOOR-YONGE
Berryman St.
Ketchum Park
Bay St.
Bellair St.
Cumberland St.
BAY
St. Thomas St.
Hazelton Ave.
Webster Ave.
Gardiner Museum of Ceramic Art
Charles St. W
Queen's Park Crescent E
St. Joseph St.
Avenue Rd.
Royal Ontario Museum
MUSEUM
Queen's Park
Tranby Ave.
Elgin Ave.
Bernard Ave.
Bedford Rd.
UNIVERSITY OF TORONTO
Prince Arthur Ave.
Lowther Ave.
Admiral Rd.
Bloor St. W.
ST. GEORGE
Devonshire Pl.
Hoskin Ave.
Barnicke Gallery
St. George St.
St. George St.
Huron St.
ANNEX
SPADINA
Bata Shoe Museum
Spadina Ave.
Walmer Rd.
Dalton Rd.
Major St.
Brunswick Ave.
Howland Ave.
Lippincott St.
Lennox St.
BATHURST

Area of map
College St.
Dundas St. E.
Queen St. W.
Yonge St.
Avenue Rd.
University Ave.
Spadina Ave.
Bathurst St.
Dupont St.
Bloor St. W.
King St. W.
Dufferin St.

The Bay 19
Bay Bloor Radio 16
Birks 17
Book City 21
Davids 13
george C 6
Goodfoot 14
Harry Rosen 12
Hazelton Lanes 1
Holt Renfrew 18
M.A.C. 11
Nicolas 4
Noor 3
Risqué 22
Roots 10
Royal de Versailles 9
Second Time Around 7
Specchio 15
Teatro Verde 8
TNT Blu 8
Trove 20
Winners 5

Downtown Shopping

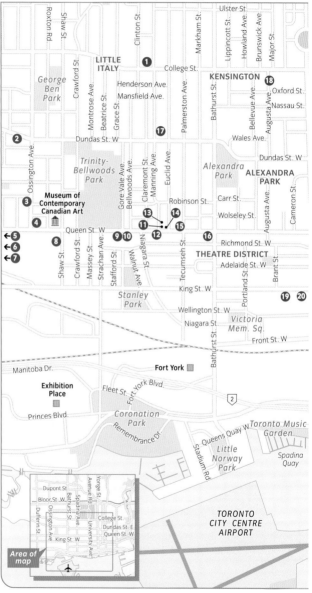

LITTLE ITALY ❶

KENSINGTON ❶❽

Roxton Rd.

Shaw St.

Crawford St.

Clinton St.

Markham St.

Ulster St.

Lippincott St.

Howland Ave.

Brunswick Ave.

Major St.

College St.

George Ben Park

Henderson Ave.

Mansfield Ave.

Montrose Ave.

Beatrice St.

Grace St.

Palmerston Ave.

Bathurst St.

Bellevue Ave.

Augusta Ave.

Oxford St.

Nassau St.

❷

Ossington Ave.

Dundas St. W.

Wales Ave.

❶❼

Trinity-Bellwoods Park

Dundas St. W.

Alexandra Park

ALEXANDRA PARK

Claremont St.

Manning Ave.

Euclid Ave.

Augusta Ave.

Cameron St.

❸ **Museum of Contemporary Canadian Art** 🏛

Robinson St.

Carr St.

Wolseley St.

❹

←❺
←❻
←❼

Queen St. W.

Gore Vale Ave.

Bellwoods Ave.

❽

❾ ❿

Niagara St.

Walnut Ave.

❶❸ ❶❹

❶❶ ❶❷ ❶❺

❶❻

Richmond St. W.

THEATRE DISTRICT

Adelaide St. W.

Portland St.

Brant St.

Shaw St.

Crawford St.

Massey St.

Strachan Ave.

Stafford St.

Tecumseh St.

Stanley Park

King St. W.

❶❾ ❷⓿

Wellington St. W.

Niagara St.

Victoria Mem. Sq.

Bathurst St.

Front St. W.

Manitoba Dr.

Fort York ▪

Exhibition Place ▪

Fleet St.

Fort York Blvd.

Coronation Park

Remembrance Dr.

Princes Blvd.

②

Queens Quay W.

Toronto Music Garden

Stadium Rd.

Little Norway Park

Spadina Quay

Area of map

Dupont St.

Bloor St. W.

Dufferin St.

Ossington Ave.

Bathurst St.

Spadina Ave.

Avenue Rd.

University Ave.

Yonge St.

College St.

Dundas St. E.

Queen St. W.

King St. W.

TORONTO CITY CENTRE AIRPORT

Toronto Shopping A to Z

Antiques

★ **Antiques at the St. Lawrence** DOWNTOWN   A hidden gem, this cozy emporium offers a mercurial selection of furniture, textiles, crockery, and other funky and shabby-chic knickknacks. Call ahead—the store's open unusual hours. *92 Front St. E.* ☎ *416/350-8865. AE, MC, V. Subway: Union (from there, walk east along Front St. for 3 blocks). Map p 77.*

★ **Filter** DOWNTOWN   Owned by the proprietors of the farther-flung Queen West Antique Centre (see "What's Old Is New," below), this is a somewhat more focused and pricey version of that store. It is stocked with tantalizing, condo-friendly, midcentury modern pieces. *75 Jarvis St.* ☎ *647/428-7265. AE, MC, V. Subway: King (from there, walk east to Jarvis). Map p 77.*

Morba QUEEN WEST   Seemingly lit with thousands of funky lamps, this jampacked temple to classic Scandinavian and American design stocks everything from repro Eames chairs to taxidermied animals. *665 Queen St. W.* ☎ *416/364-5144. AE, MC, V. Subway: Osgoode, then 501 streetcar west. Map p 77.*

Toronto Antiques on King ENTERTAINMENT DISTRICT   While the vast majority of the city's antiques shops lie outside the downtown core (see "What's Old Is New," below), this large building is a good one-stop shop, housing a wide array of dealers specializing in high-end jewelry, art, and carpets. *276 King St. W.* ☎ *416/345-9941. AE, MC, V. Subway: St. Andrew. Map p 77.*

Books

Book City ANNEX   A local indie chain with outlets across downtown, this store's motto is "comfortable, classy and cheap." It's also open late—a good place to grab a newspaper from back home when you're struggling with jet lag. *501 Bloor St. W.* ☎ *416/961-4496. MC, V. Subway: Spadina. Map p 78.*

★ **Chapters** ENTERTAINMENT DISTRICT   One of the main downtown locations for Canada's largest book

GUFF is one of several great antique stores on Queen Street East.

Type has quickly become one of the city's most beloved booksellers.

retailer, this 3-story store is hard to beat for selection. With a Starbucks and music section in-house, and the Scotiabank Theatre multiplex next door, you can easily pass many hours here. *126 John St.* ☎ *416/595-7349. AE, MC, V. Subway: Osgoode, then walk 3 blocks west to John. Map p 77.*

★★ **Good Egg** KENSINGTON MARKET As sweet as its name-sake, this bookstore-cum-kitchen supply shop doesn't sell food, but it'll sure whet your appetite. An imaginative selection of books is complemented by witty gift items, utensils, and cookware. *267 Augusta Ave.* ☎ *416/593-4663. AE, MC, V. Subway: Queen's Park, then 506 streetcar west to Augusta and walk a block south. Map p 77.*

★★ **The Monkey's Paw** DUNDAS WEST This cabinet of curiosities is the city's most eccentric secondhand bookshop. Specializing in oddball scholarly texts and ephemera, it's

What's Old Is New

Toronto's great antiques shops are scattered in various pockets around the city, adding further challenge for the visiting scavenger. One simple way to get a sense of available bargains is to start at one end of Queen Street West and make your way east by streetcar and foot to the booming neighborhood of **Leslieville.** On Queen West, at Roncesvalles, you'll be in **Parkdale,** home to the bustling **Queen West Antique Centre** (1605 Queen St. W.; ☎ 416/588-2212) and **Era** (1629 Queen St. W.; ☎ 416/535-3305), a small shop with a penchant for Americana. East of Yonge, Leslieville's many charms include midcentury modern experts **Zig Zag** (1142 Queen St. E.; ☎ 416/778-6495), old-timers **Elbers Antiques and Refinishing** (777 Queen St. E.; ☎ 416/466-3938) and **GUFF** (1152 Queen St. E.; ☎ 416/913-8025), which stands for good, used furniture finds.

also one of the best places to find an antique typewriter. *1229 Dundas St. W. ☎ 416/531-2123. MC, V. Subway: Ossington (from there, take the 63 Ossington bus south to Dundas). Map p 77.*

★★ **Swipe** QUEEN WEST A haven for design geeks, this well-appointed store carries a wide array of books and magazines on branding, advertising, architecture, and urbanism. A gorgeous assortment of well-designed housewares, ceramics, and wooden toys round out the offerings. *401 Richmond St. W. ☎ 416/363-1332. MC, V. Subway: Osgoode. Map p 77.*

★★★ **Type** WEST QUEEN WEST Adorable and friendly, this shop has quickly become one of the most-beloved booksellers in the city. The small children's section is well stocked with hard-to-find titles and there's even a section for "plotless fiction" (think Samuel Beckett). *883 Queen St. W. ☎ 416/366-8973. AE, MC, V. Subway: Osgoode, then 501 streetcar west. Map p 77.*

Cosmetics
M.A.C. BLOOR STREET It got its start in Toronto in 1985 and now this cosmetics giant has shops around the world. In Toronto, the flagship on Bloor is the biggest and busiest, selling more than 200 foundation colors alone. Make-up lessons are available. *89 Bloor St. W. ☎ 416/929-7555. AE, MC, V. Subway: Bay. Map p 78.*

★★★ **Noor** YORKVILLE This stylish perfume emporium, in the basement of the Four Seasons Hotel, carries a well-curated array of scents, from such exclusive houses as Penhaligon's and L'Artisan Parfumeur. The proprietors offer expert, gentle guidance for the fragrance newbie. *176 Cumberland St. ☎ 416/928-0700. AE, MC, V. Subway: Bay. Map p 78.*

Department Stores
The Bay BLOOR STREET Practically synonymous with Canadian retail, this is the country's oldest department store. The selection is somewhat staid—and this flagship store is a grim, gray fortress—but it's still a good spot to pick up basics, which are almost always on sale. *44 Bloor St. E. ☎ 416/972-3333. AE, MC, V. Subway: Yonge. Map p 78.*

The staff at Noors offers expert guidance on fragrances.

★ **Harry Rosen** BLOOR STREET
Canada's biggest menswear store
got even bigger in 2008, undergoing
a dramatic $20-million renovation.
Now five stories tall, it carries even
more of the Brioni suits, Etro shirts,
and Ferragamo shoes the shop is
known for. *77 Bloor St. W.* ☎ *416/
935-9200. AE, MC, V. Subway: Bay.
Map p 78.*

★ **Holt Renfrew** BLOOR STREET
Like its international kissing cousins
Harrods and Barneys, Holt specializes in high-end fashion and loads of
attitude. But if it's Marc Jacobs or
Balenciaga you're after, this is the
place to go. Frequent sales take
some of the sting out of the prices.
50 Bloor St. W. ☎ *416/922-2333. AE,
MC, V. Subway: Bay. Map p 78.*

Winners BLOOR STREET   Dis-
counted brand-name apparel (often
60% off retail), but finding the diamonds in the rough requires great
reserves of persistence. *110 Bloor St.
W.* ☎ *416/920-0193. AE, MC, V. Subway: Bay. Map p 77.*

Electronics
★★★ **Bay Bloor Radio** BLOOR
STREET   An audiophile's dream,
this elegant showroom carries cutting-edge stereo and video equipment—and a staff knowledgeable
enough to properly talk about it. *55
Bloor St. W.* ☎ *416/967-1122. AE,
MC, V. Subway: Bay. Map p 78.*

Fashion
★ **Comrags** WEST QUEEN WEST
Queen West fashion icons, the design
duo of Joyce Gunhouse and Judy Cor-
nish are renowned for their classic but
edgy collections, designed to accommodate all body types. *654 Queen St.
W.* ☎ *416/360-7249. AE, MC, V. Subway: Osgoode, then 501 streetcar
west. Map p 77.*

★ **Fresh Collective** WEST QUEEN
WEST   This somewhat chaotic shop

*Holt Renfrew specializes in high-end
fashion.*

and studio features dozens of different local designers, who produce
everything from whimsical, one-of-
a-kind children's clothing to smart,
trendy womenswear. *692 Queen St.
W.* ☎ *416/594-1313. MC, V. Subway: Osgoode, then 501 streetcar
west. Map p 77.*

george C YORKVILLE   Housed in
a serene, renovated Yorkville Victorian, this unisex boutique carries a
range of coveted, exclusive designers from the likes of Neil Barrett and
Costume National. *21 Hazelton Ave.*
☎ *416/962-1991. AE, MC, V. Subway: Bay. Map p 78.*

Gotstyle ENTERTAINMENT DIS-
TRICT   This menswear shop is
proudly, strenuously masculine—
from the on-site mens-only spa to
the b-ball-broadcasting flatscreen
TVs. Labels run the gamut from John
Varvatos to Earnest Sewn. *489 King
St. W.* ☎ *416/260-9696. AE, MC, V.
Subway: St. Andrew. Map p 77.*

★ **GreenShag** WEST QUEEN WEST
Famous for its whimsical designs—
cufflinks in the shape of hockey rinks,
French cuffs printed with wine lists—
this bespoke men's clothier can jazz
up the most lackluster wardrobe. *670
Queen St. W.* ☎ *416/360-7424. AE,
MC, V. Subway: Osgoode, then 501
streetcar west. Map p 77.*

Sydney's is an elegant menswear shop popular with artists.

★ **Jonathan and Olivia** WEST QUEEN WEST   Friendly staff and funky clothing (hip stuff from APC and Helmut Lang, among others) make this Ossington hot spot, the only clothing outlet in a strip of bars and galleries, a destination. *49 Ossington Ave.* ☎ *416/849-5956. AE, MC, V. Subway: Ossington, then 63 bus south. Map p 77.*

Klaxon Howl WEST QUEEN WEST   Tucked away in a laneway coach house just north of Queen and specializing in hypermasculine vintage and military-inspired menswear, this is the hipster's Army & Navy. *694 Queen St. W. (rear entrance)* ☎ *647/436-6628. AE, MC, V. Subway: Osgoode, then 501 streetcar west. Map p 77.*

Lileo DISTILLERY   Named for Galileo, this large unisex lifestyle boutique has the feel of an upscale Urban Outfitters but the social conscience of a Lululemon. Fair-trade labels and fabrics abound. *55 Mill St.* ☎ *416/413-1410. AE, MC, V. Subway: Castle Frank, then 65A Parliament St. bus to Mill St. Map p 77.*

Nicolas YORKVILLE   Old-world service complements the impeccably

cut creations (by Paul Smith, Canali, and others) at this temple to sartorial splendor. Menswear's in one half, women's in the other, and both are popular with the business people and condo dwellers who live and work in the area. *153 Cumberland St.* ☎ *416/966-2064. AE, MC, V. Subway: Bay. Map p 78.*

★★ **Preloved** WEST QUEEN WEST   Original, unique women's clothing created from reclaimed vintage fabrics. Popular with visiting starlets like Anne Hathaway and Kate Hudson. *881 Queen St. W.* ☎ *416/504-8704. AE, MC, V. Subway: Osgoode, then 501 streetcar west. Map p 77.*

★ **Risqué** ANNEX   This adorable womenswear boutique has long been a favorite with trendsetters. It can be pricey but the pieces—from labels like Bionic and Dish—are expertly selected and showcased. *404 Bloor St. W.* ☎ *416/960-3325. AE, MC, V. Subway: Spadina. Map p 78.*

Roots BLOOR STREET   While some of its popularity might have waned, this familiar Canadian stalwart nonetheless continues to turn out decent leather goods, reliable sweats, and ecochic yoga wear. *100 Bloor St. W.*

☎ *416/323-3289. AE, MC, V. Subway: Bay. Map p 78.*

★★★ **Sydney's** WEST QUEEN WEST   An elegant, discerning menswear shop, popular with trendsetters and artists. Bespoke jeans, cut from rare Japanese denim, are a special treat, as is owner Sydney Mamane's own line of shirts. *795 Queen St. W.* ☎ *416/603-3369. AE, MC, V. Subway: Osgoode, then 501 streetcar west. Map p 77.*

TNT Blu YORKVILLE   The sassy, youthful branch of the TNT minichain (the names stands for The New Trend) carries a wide—and pricey—range of street fashion for men and women. *Hazelton Lanes, 55 Avenue Rd.* ☎ *416/972-1593. AE, MC, V. Subway: Bay. Map p 78.*

★ **Virginia Johnson** WEST QUEEN WEST   This local designer is beloved for her summery floral frocks, inventive textiles (with imagery usually derived from nature), and charming bags and throw pillows. *132 Ossington Ave.* ☎ *416/516-3366. MC, V. Subway: Ossington 63 bus south from Ossington. Map p 77.*

Furniture

Design Within Reach DOWNTOWN   All the icons—Eames rockers, Saarinen tables and more—can be in found in this 437sq.-m (4,700-sq.-ft.) store, the only Canadian outpost of the San Francisco–based chain of modern design stores. *435 King St. W.* ☎ *416/977-4003. AE, MC, V. Subway: St. Andrew, then 504 King streetcar west. Map p 77.*

★★ **MADE** DUNDAS WEST   This is a wonderland of locally made, cutting-edge furniture and accessories. Many of the unique and eccentric pieces are composed of ecofriendly materials and an exhibition space in the back—the MADE Cooler—further emphasizes the high-art aspect of the products. *867 Dundas St. W.* ☎ *416/607-6384. AE, MC, V. Subway: Bathurst, then 511 streetcar south to Dundas and walk west 2 blocks. Map p 77.*

Gifts

★ **Bergo** DISTILLERY   An enormous shrine to fine design, this is the perfect place for finding unique gifts—from kitchen utensils to one-of-a-kind writing instruments. Products are designed by all the heavy hitters, from Frank Gehry to Philippe Starck. *55 Mill St.* ☎ *416/861-1821. AE, MC, V. Subway: Castle Frank, then 65A Parliament bus south to Mill St. Map p 77.*

★ **Drake General Store** WEST QUEEN WEST   Tucked in beside the famed boutique hotel, this is a great spot to pick up unique Canadiana to take back home. You'll find everything from a Moleskine Toronto notebook to canvas bags imprinted with the Mounties' logo. *1144 Queen St. W.* ☎ *416/531-5042. AE, MC, V. Subway: Osgoode, then 501 streetcar west. Map p 77.*

Design Within Reach carries many of the iconic names of modern furniture design.

Studio Brillantine features items with eye-catching design.

★★ Studio Brillantine WEST QUEEN WEST   Where this cute, provocative store goes, the art and design community follows—a relocation last year to deep Parkdale signaled that neighborhood's further gentrification. Gorgeously designed cookware sits next to museum-quality toys and some of the coolest greeting cards around. *1518 Queen St. W.* ☎ *416/536-6521. AE, MC, V. Subway: Osgoode, then 501 streetcar west. Map p 77.*

★★ Teatro Verde YORKVILLE   Recently relocated to a huge

neo-Georgian mansion, the flagship of this upscale gardening and home emporium stocks exceptional gifts, like Kate Spade's hurricane lamps and cute OOTS! lunchboxes. *100 Yorkville Ave.* ☎ *416/966-2227. AE, MC, V. Subway: Bay. Map p 78.*

Jewelry

★ Birks BLOOR STREET   Looking for diamonds mined in Canada? This is the place. Birks is a Canadian institution and its Toronto flagship consists of two floors of crystal, watches, pearl necklaces, antique estate jewelry, and baby gifts. *55 Bloor St. W.* ☎ *416/922-2266. AE, MC, V. Subway: Bay. Map p 78.*

Royal de Versailles YORKVILLE   This is the go-to place for watches at heart-stopping prices. Your run-of-the-mill Rolexes can be had here, of course—they have Canada's largest selection—but timepiece connoisseurs come for the Audemars Piguet and Girard-Perregaux. *101 Bloor St. W.* ☎ *416/967-7201. AE, MC, V. Subway: Bay. Map p 78.*

★ Trove ANNEX   This cute boutique attracts a similarly attractive clientele. Carrying an eclectic array of clothing, footwear, and accessories,

Trove has an eclectic array of clothing, footwear, and accessories from local and international designers.

The Eaton Centre is the largest and best-known downtown shopping centre in the city.

it does a brisk business in eccentric earrings and necklaces from local and international designers. *793 Bathurst St. ☎ 416/516-1258. AE, MC, V. Subway: Bathurst. Map p 78.*

Malls

Eaton Centre DOWNTOWN
Unfortunately, this is often the only shopping destination that many tourists see. But this immense downtown mall and landmark does contain such staples as H+M, Club Monaco, and Apple. Alas, no more Eaton's—the Canadian department store that gave the center its name went bankrupt in 1999. *220 Yonge St. ☎ 416/598-8700. Subway: Dundas. Map p 77.*

Hazelton Lanes YORKVILLE
Even though a revitalized Bloor Street has stolen some of this high-end mall's thunder, it still boasts dozens of exclusive shops, spas, and restaurants. Some luxe highlights: footwear chain Browns, Andrew's (best known for its vast Burberry selection), and Hugo Nicholson, purveyor of ultrachic gowns by Carolina Herrera and others. *87 Avenue Rd. ☎ 416/968-8680. Subway: Bay. Map p 78.*

Music

Play de Record DOWNTOWN
Superstar DJ Jason Palma owns this

record and DJ equipment shop, which naturally caters to turntablists from all over North America. *357A Yonge St. ☎ 416/586-0380. AE, MC, V. Subway: Dundas. Map p 77.*

★★★ Soundscapes COLLEGE STREET This is a beloved hangout of many a local musician and the best CD shop in town if your taste runs to the indie, the obscure, and the alternative. The compelling selection is organized by genre and label and there are helpful listening posts stocked with favorite new releases. *572 College St. ☎ 416/537-1620. MC, V. Subway: Queen's Park, then 506 streetcar west. Map p 77.*

Shoes

★ Davids BLOOR STREET A multi-million-dollar renovation in 2008 made this footwear fantasyland even more beguiling. The most exclusive brands for men and women are all here—Christian Louboutin, Marc Jacobs, and Casadei—and the knowledgeable staff wait on you hand and, yes, foot. *66 Bloor St. W. ☎ 416/920-1000. AE, MC, V. Subway: Bay. Map p 78.*

Goodfoot YORKVILLLE The it spot for rare and very expensive sneakers, this hyperhip boutique is the place to pick up fluorescent

Davids carries some of the most exclusive brands in men's and women's footwear.

Gore-Tex New Balances, Nike Dunks, Skupra Sky Tops, and other exclusive models. *1200 Bay St.* ☎ *647/430-5887. AE, MC, V. Subway: Bay. Map p 78.*

★ **John Fluevog** QUEEN WEST Notorious for his playful, offbeat designs, this local footwear fave turns out clogs, brogues, and boots that you can imagine a Goth-minded Betty Boop wearing. (Or Madonna or Rihanna, who are fans.) *242 Queen St. W.* ☎ *416/581-1420. AE, MC, V. Subway: Osgoode. Map p 77.*

Specchio YORKVILLE Shoebox-size but packed with rare and unusual European treasures, this shop offers adventurous designs by Dries Van Noten and Costume National. *1240 Bay St.* ☎ *416/961-7989. AE, MC, V. Subway: Bay. Map p 78.*

Toys

★★ **Ella and Elliot** WEST QUEEN WEST Even adults get a kick out of this inviting furniture and toy boutique. Most of the stock is European made, sustainable, and modern and the well-crafted, high-end toys and games appeal to children of all ages. *188 Strachan Ave.* ☎ *416/850-7890. AE, MC, V. Subway: Osgoode, then*

501 streetcar west to Strachan. Map p 77.

Vintage Fashion

Black Market QUEEN WEST No wardrobe's complete without an old-school Ramones T-shirt. Skip the Blue Jays memorabilia and get a souvenir from the "megawarehouse" of this legendary vintage minichain. *256A Queen St. W.* ☎ *416/599-5858. MC, V. Subway: Osgoode. Map p 77.*

Second Time Around YORKVILLE Deep in the heart of Yorkville lies a bargain hunter's dream. Especially if that bargain hunter is a label queen. This consignment shop carries the finest in women's clothing—from Chanel to Prada—all at an unbelievable discount. *111 Yorkville Ave.* ☎ *416/916-7669. AE, MC, V. Subway: Bay. Map p 78.*

★ **69 Vintage** WEST QUEEN WEST Given the artful arrangement of the clothes in this shop, you might think you've accidentally wandered into a Queen West gallery. Dig deeper, however, and you'll find some of the coolest bargains in town, from vintage tracksuits to excellent footwear. *1100 Queen St. W.* ☎ *416/516-0669. MC, V. Subway: Osgoode, then 501 streetcar west. Map p 77.* ●

5 The **Great Outdoors**

High Park

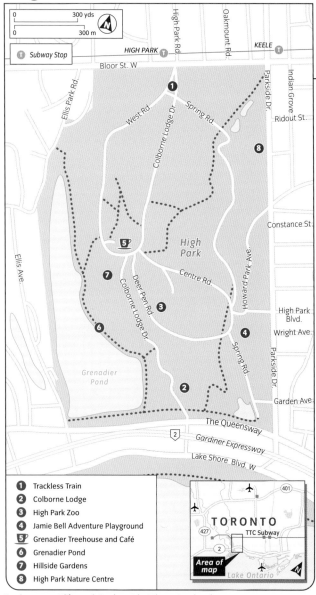

0 300 yds
0 300 m

N

🚇 Subway Stop

HIGH PARK 🚇

Bloor St. W

Ellis Park Rd.

West Rd.

Colborne Lodge Dr.

Spring Rd.

High Park Rd.

Oakmount Rd.

KEELE 🚇

Parkside Dr.

Indian Grove

Ridout St.

❶

❽

Constance St.

Ellis Ave.

5 🍵

❼

High Park

Centre Rd.

❸

Deer Pen Rd.

Colborne Lodge Dr.

Howard Park Ave.

High Park Blvd.

❹

Wright Ave.

Parkside Dr.

❻

Grenadier Pond

❷

Spring Rd.

Garden Ave.

The Queensway

2

Gardiner Expressway

Lake Shore Blvd. W

❶ Trackless Train
❷ Colborne Lodge
❸ High Park Zoo
❹ Jamie Bell Adventure Playground
5 Grenadier Treehouse and Café
❻ Grenadier Pond
❼ Hillside Gardens
❽ High Park Nature Centre

✈

401

TORONTO

427

TTC Subway

2

Area of map

Lake Ontario

N

Previous page: A lifeguard stands watch at the eastern beaches.

On the signs for its hundreds of green spaces, Toronto is described as a "city within a park." This feels most true when strolling through High Park, downtown's largest natural enclave. At almost 162 hectares (400 acres), the hilly park is an isolated but easily accessible idyll where nature buffs, sports enthusiasts, and families enjoy a bountiful blend of manicured gardens, bucolic attractions, and untamed wilderness. START: **High Park Station.**

The trackless train provides a scenic 25-minute ride through High Park.

1 kids **Trackless Train.** The best way to get your bearings is to take this charming, 25-minute-long train ride, which weaves slowly throughout the park. (The "train" is basically a tractor that pulls along two wagons.) Purchase tickets from the train operator. ⏱ ½ hr. ☎ 647/438-007. Tickets *$4 adults, $3 seniors 60 and over and children. Apr 1–30 and Sept 11–Oct 31 Sat–Sun 10:30am–dusk; May 1–Sept 10 daily 10:30am–dusk.*

2 ★ kids **Colborne Lodge.** The original High Park was founded in 1876 by John George Howard, one of the city's first architects, and his wife, Jemima. Their secluded, Regency-style cottage was built in 1837 (becoming part of the park in 1890), and it now serves as one of Toronto's 10 historic museums, allowing visitors full enjoyment of its original furnishings, gardens, and artifacts. ⏱ *1 hr.* ☎ *416/392-6916.*

The Colborne Lodge museum was originally the home of High Park's founder.

Admission $5.71 (+tax) adults; $2.62 (regular admission) $3.81 (mid-Nov to Jan) seniors 65 and over and youth 13–18; $2.38 (regular) $3.33 (mid-Nov to Jan) children 4–12. Mid-Jan, Feb, and April Fri–Sat noon–4pm; Mar Thurs–Sun noon–4pm; Mar break Mon–Sun noon–4pm; May–Aug Tues–Sun noon–5pm; Sept Sat–Sun noon–5pm; Oct–Dec Tues–Sun noon–4pm; Christmas Eve and New Year's Eve noon–3pm.

❸ ★ **kids High Park Zoo.** Beginning with deer in 1890, High Park has long kept domesticated and wild animals in its paddocks. Today, the small zoo, tucked away in a shady ravine, is one of the park's most popular attractions (albeit one in dire need of renovation). Dozens of different exotic and indigenous animals, from wallabies to peacocks, are on hand. Caution, though: the animals may be cute, but this isn't a petting zoo. ⏲ ½ hr. *Free admission. Daily 7am–dusk.*

❹ ★★ **kids Jamie Bell Adventure Playground.** A munchkin's paradise, this volunteer-built playground, designed to reflect local architecture and natural beauty, boasts a unique system of castle turrets, monkey bars, and dozens of different slides. Grown-ups will be

The Jamie Bell Adventure Playground is a kids' paradise.

hard-pressed to resist an occasional trip down one of the slides. ⏲ 1 hr. *Free admission. Daily 7am–dusk.*

❺ ★ **Grenadier Teahouse and Café.** If a picnic's not an option, this centrally located cafe is a quaint, well-priced alternative. The requisite burgers and ice cream are

Play Date

Every July and August for the past 25 years, the Canadian Stage Company has brought open-air theater to High Park. The **Dream in High Park** (www.canstage.com) specializes in Shakespeare. Plays produced have included, naturally, *A Midsummer Night's Dream*—but a Canadian classic is occasionally performed. Admission is pay-what-you-can. Before Sunday performances, families can go backstage for free arts and crafts, tours of the set, and acting workshops. In mid-July, the stage is turned over to the **Scream in High Park** (www.thescream.ca), an eclectic literary festival that has now expanded to the entire city and lasts a whole week.

Hoofing It

Not surprisingly, the best way to get around High Park is on foot. The Spring Creek and West Ravine nature trails are long and labyrinthine (though clearly marked) and allow you to fully experience the park's wildlife. Walking tours are hosted by the High Park Citizen's Advisory Committee (www.highpark.org) throughout the year. In winter, the trails are perfect for cross-country skiing, although skiers are also permitted the full run of the park.

offered and complete breakfasts and wood-fired, oven-cooked pizzas are also available. (Alcohol, however, is not available.) While there's plenty of seating inside and out, the place is packed on weekends and holidays. Enter from Bloor St. gate, follow the main road toward the center of the park. ☎ 416/769-9870. $.

⑥ ★ kids Grenadier Pond. This small, inland lake feeds right into Lake Ontario and is one of the park's most picturesque spots. While neither boating nor ice skating are permitted anymore, anglers can often be found first thing in the morning, enjoying some tranquil shoreline fishing. The lake is home to carp, pike, bass, and, supposedly, large snapping turtles. Fishing licenses can be obtained by calling ☎ 416/314-2000.

⑦ Hillside Gardens. Horticulturalists will marvel at the landscaped splendor of this miniature Eden, comprised of three, distinct areas: the Hillside Gardens, the Hanging Gardens, and the Sunken Gardens. While wedding photography is forbidden, shutterbugs are welcome to take snaps. ⏱ 30 min. Free admission. 7 am–dusk daily.

⑧ kids High Park Nature Centre. Get the park's abundant flora and fauna explained to you at this helpful volunteer education center. The center runs informative walking tours, botanical classes, and day camps for kids. *Free, naturalist-led walking tours are held every second and fourth Sunday, starting at 10:30am, and last an hour and a half. Program prices vary but start at $5; check www.highpark.org for more information. Call for hours.* ☎ 416/392-1748.

Grenadier Pond is perfect for tranquil, shoreline fishing.

The Toronto Islands

1 Centreville
2 Toronto Island Bicycle Rental
3 The Rectory Café
4 Hanlan's Point
5 Ward's Island

Take a short ferry ride from downtown and you'll find yourself in a serene, verdant, care-free paradise. While 14 separate islands make up this small archipelago in the city's harbor, locals commonly refer to the whole area as the Island. Developed as a park in the late '50s—boasting numerous beaches, bike paths, tennis courts, and an amusement park—the Island is also home to about 600 feisty full-time residents. START: **Ferries leave every 15 minutes from docks at the foot of Bay Street.**

---

1 kids **Centreville.** This may not be the most spectacular amusement park, but it's definitely the most convenient and attractive. The 30 different rides and attractions include such traditional treats as a Ferris wheel and roller coaster as well as horseback rides and the idiosyncratic Haunted Barrel Works. A couple of decent restaurants serve visitors and there are numerous picnic spots. ⏲ *2 hr. Centre Island.* ☎ *416/203-0405. Free admission.*

Ride tickets start at 85¢. Family pass for four $90 (includes unlimited rides). June 1–Sept 1 daily 10:30am–8pm; May and Sept Sat–Sun weather permitting.

2 kids **Toronto Island Bicycle Rental.** Strolling around the Island is a delight, but you'll get a greater sense of its treasures by exploring the 10km (6.2 miles) of trails that span the three main islands by bike. ⏲ *2 hr. Centre Island Pier.*

Cycling is one of the best ways to get around the Toronto Islands.

☎ *416/203-0009. Single and tandem bicycles ($6–$13/hr); two- and four-seat quadricycles ($16–$28/hr).*

3⃣ ★★ The Rectory Café. This tearoom and restaurant, originally built in the 19th century, offers one of the city's quaintest dining experiences. Grab a spot on the garden patio and nibble on sammies and salads or a more substantial seafood meal. *102 Lakeshore Ave., Ward's Island.* ☎ *416/203-2152. $$.*

4⃣ ★ Hanlan's Point. The city's only clothing-optional beach, situated on the western side of the Island, is nicely secluded. A popular spot for outgoing gay men, its silky sand also attracts families. Baseball buffs: Babe Ruth hit his first professional home run in the Hanlan's Point stadium. It was demolished to make way for the controversial Island Airport.

5⃣ Ward's Island. The Island's defiantly independent residents are concentrated almost entirely in the car-free Algonquin and Ward's Island communities, crowded into around 250 small, cottage homes. The houses range from the adorably fairy-tale-like to the ramshackle, and walking through the narrow streets will give you insight into a unique community. Home ownership here is strictly regulated: Islanders pay the city to lease their lots and can only pass on homes to spouses or children.

Paddlers Paradise

A unique—and very Canadian—way to experience the Island's waterways is to hop in a canoe or kayak and paddle over. The Harbourfront Canoe & Kayak Club rents both types of watercraft (starting at $30/hr.), with all safety equipment, taxes, and a map included in the price. Make your way across the Western Gap shipping channel, skirt around the airport, and head to the still backwaters within the Islands, where you'll find a rarely seen bird sanctuary.

The Beach

1. Ashbridge's Bay Park
2. Woodbine Beach
3. D.D. Summerville Pool
4. Lick's
5. Glen Stewart Park
6. Kew Gardens
7. The Martin Goodman Trail

A 2006 poll led to The Beaches being rebranded with a singular sobriquet, although this glorious east-end neighborhood, 15 minutes from downtown, sits on three distinct beaches. Swimming can be iffy—call the Beach Water Quality Hotline (☎ 416/392-7161) before donning your flippers—but the long strip of sand offers ample space for sunbathing, kite flying, volleyball, and Frisbee. Strollers can enjoy the sunset from the 3km (1.7-mile) boardwalk. START: **Queen Street East streetcar to Woodbine.**

① ★★ kids Ashbridge's Bay Park. Named for an American Quaker who settled here in 1793, the 35-hectare (86-acre) waterfront park adjoining Woodbine Beach is largely devoted to sporting activities—softball diamonds, rugby fields, and a public marina are all on hand. The rocky shoreline and wooded footpaths make for delightful exploration. *Lakeshore Blvd. E. (just east of Coxwell Ave.).*

② kids Woodbine Beach. The place to see and be seen, this sandy strip attracts sun worshipers, randy teenagers, and well-oiled beach volleyball players. Various sporting events are regularly held here, including Heatwave, the city's

Woodbine Beach is a hot spot for beach volleyball.

largest beach volleyball tournament, a benefit for the Sick Kids Hospital. *1675 Lakeshore Blvd. E.*

③ kids D.D. Summerville Pool. If Lake Ontario's E. coli levels are too high, this free public pool offers a refreshing alternative. There are actually three pools: a 50-meter Olympic-size pool, a 25-meter kiddie pool, and a diving pool with two boards. The whole complex is set about three stories above ground, offering spectacular views of the city and lake. *1675 Lakeshore Blvd. E. ☎ 416/3392-7688. Hours vary; call for details.*

④ Lick's. This beloved local chain is famous for its burgers and shakes, but also for the songs (charming to some, annoying to others) that its staff breaks into every time an order is placed. *1960 Queen St. E. ☎ 416/362-5425. $.*

⑤ ★ Glen Stewart Park. While the waterfront is obviously the main attraction, this 75-hectare (185-acre) ravine park, just steps from the main drag, is a favorite with birdwatchers and hikers. Peak time for observing migrating songbirds is mid-May. *Queen St. E. and Glen Manor Dr.*

⑥ ★ kids Kew Gardens. This quaint public park stretches from the bustling boutiques of Queen East to the waterfront. Formerly a small amusement park, it's now used

Beaches International Jazz Festival

The Kew Gardens bandstand is the main stage venue for the Beaches International Jazz Festival (www.beachesjazz.com). This popular—and entirely free—20-year-old music festival is held every July. The fest takes place over 10 days at venues throughout the neighborhood. Hundreds of local and international artists—such as Elizabeth Shepard, Dr. Draw, Hilario Duran, and Jane Bunnett—dazzle about a million sun-struck jazz fans each year. A lecture and workshop series is also offered for aspiring musicians. *Admission is free.*

The 20-year-old Beaches International Jazz Fest attracts a million fans over 10 days.

primarily for picnics, lawn bowling, tennis, and softball games. A water pad and wading pool help keep the kiddies cool. One of the few remaining historical buildings is the iconic Leuty Avenue Lifeguard Station, restored in 1993. *2075 Queen St. E.*

7 ★★★ kids **The Martin Goodman Trail.** A 900km-long (559-mile) waterfront trail runs along Lake Ontario and the St. Lawrence River, from Niagara-on-the-Lake to the border of Quebec. The Toronto section of this trail runs from the western edge of the city to the beaches, wending its way through cityscapes, beaches, and woods. A glorious way to see the city. Directions and maps are available on the website. *www.waterfronttrail.org.* ●

6 The Best **Dining**

Dining Best Bets

Best **Desserts**
★★ Mistura $$$$ *265 Davenport Rd. (p 110)*

Best **Local Wine List**
★ Frank $$ *317 Dundas St. W. (p 107)*

Best **Deluxe Burger**
★ Bymark $$$$ *66 Wellington St. W. (p 104)*

Best **Patio**
★★ Grace $$ *503 College St. (p 108)*

Most **Romantic**
★★ Amuse-Bouche $$$ *96 Tecumseth St. (p 104)*

Best **Vegetarian**
★ Fresh $ *894 Queen St. W. (p 107)*

Best **Dinner Deal**
Utopia $ *586 College St. (p 112)*

Best **Friendly Service**
★ Addis Ababa $ *1184 Queen St. W. (p 104)*

Best **Brunch**
★ The Drake $$$ *1150 Queen St. W. (p 106)*

Best **Steak**
Barberian's $$$$ *7 Elm St. (p 104)*

Best **Authentic Pizza**
★★ Terroni $$ *57A Adelaide St. E. (p 112)*

Best **Comfort Food**
The Harbord Room $$$ *89 Harbord St. (p 108)*

Best **Place for Business Lunch**
★★★ Canoe $$$$$ *66 Wellington St. W. (p 105)*

Best **Dim Sum**
★★ Lai Wah Heen $$$ *108 Chestnut St. (p 109)*

Best **Place to See and Be Seen**
★ One $$$ *116 Yorkville Ave. (p 111)*

Best **Place for Meat Lovers**
Black Hoof $$ *928 Dundas St. W. (p 104)*

Best **Original Cuisine**
★ Colborne Lane $$$ *45 Colborne St. (p 106)*

Amuse-Bouche is one of the city's most romantic restaurants.

Previous page: The wine cellar at Bymark.

Midtown Dining

Downtown Dining

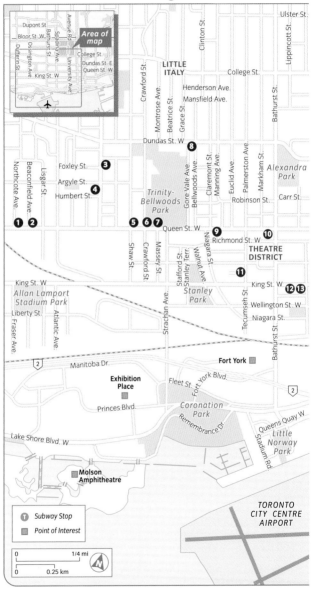

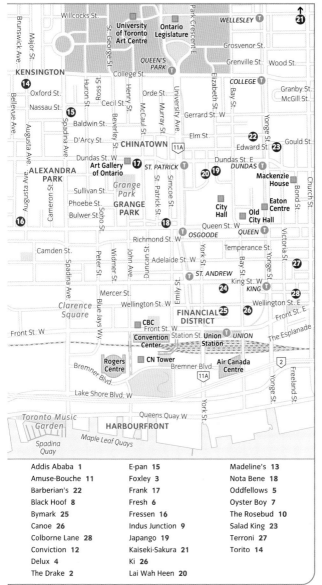

Addis Ababa **1**	E-pan **15**	Madeline's **13**
Amuse-Bouche **11**	Foxley **3**	Nota Bene **18**
Barberian's **22**	Frank **17**	Oddfellows **5**
Black Hoof **8**	Fresh **6**	Oyster Boy **7**
Bymark **25**	Fressen **16**	The Rosebud **10**
Canoe **26**	Indus Junction **9**	Salad King **23**
Colborne Lane **28**	Japango **19**	Terroni **27**
Conviction **12**	Kaiseki-Sakura **21**	Torito **14**
Delux **4**	Ki **26**	
The Drake **2**	Lai Wah Heen **20**	

Toronto Dining A to Z

★ **kids** **Addis Ababa** WEST QUEEN WEST *ETHIOPIAN* Long before the Drake and the Gladstone made this stretch of Queen hipster central, the boisterous Addis Ababa was a destination. Perfectly tangy and authentic *injera* (bread) and richly spiced meats and veggies are served here. The coffee's great too. *1184 Queen St. W.* ☎ *416/538-0059. Entrees $8–$15. MC, V. Dinner Tues–Sun. Subway: Osgoode, then 501 streetcar west. Map p 102.*

★★ **Amuse-Bouche** KING WEST *FRENCH* This is the coziest *boîte* in town, just south of the small gallery row between Queen and King. Traditional Continental dishes are enlivened with local ingredients and the desserts are to die for. *96 Tecumseth St.* ☎ *416/913-5830. Reservations recommended. Entrees $24–$29, chef tasting menu $95. AE, DC, MC, V. Dinner Tues–Sat. Streetcar: 504 King streetcar from St. Andrew (get off at Tecumseth, walk north 1 block). Map p 102.*

Barberian's DOWNTOWN *STEAKHOUSE* Now 50 years old, this old-school steakhouse is renowned for the Canadian art hung on the walls, the vast wine cellar (over 2,000 different bottles comprise the list), and, of course, its thick, dry-aged slabs of meat. *7 Elm St.* ☎ *416/597-0335. Reservations recommended. Entrees $26–$55. AE, DC, MC, V. Lunch Mon–Fri, dinner daily. Subway: Dundas. Map p 102.*

Black Hoof DUNDAS WEST *BISTRO* Charcuterie took Toronto by storm a couple years back and this petite spot has devoted itself entirely to that carnivorous, nose-to-tail craze. The small plates feature everything from venison bresaola to duck confit sandwiches. *928 Dundas St. W.* ☎ *416/551-8854. Entrees $8–$20. AE, MC, V. Dinner Thurs–Mon. Streetcar: 505 Dundas streetcar from St. Patrick. Map p 102.*

★ **Bymark** DOWNTOWN *FUSION* Best known for its $35 burger, this

Cozy Amuse-Bouche features local ingredients and to-die-for desserts.

Bymark is a magnet for the city's power brokers.

sleek restaurant (designed by Yabu Pushelberg) attracts the city's most powerful legal and financial players. The seasonally shifting menu is long on artisanal meat and unusual seafood. *66 Wellington St. W.* ☎ *416/ 777-1144. Reservations recommended. Entrees $25–$55. AE, DC, MC, V. Lunch & dinner Mon–Sat. Subway: St. Andrew. Map p 102.*

★★★ **Canoe** DOWNTOWN *FUSION* Considered by many to be Toronto's best dining experience, this restaurant in the clouds (it sits atop the TD Bank Tower) specializes in regional Canadian cuisine. Depending on the season, that can be anything from succulent Alberta lamb loin to Qualicum Beach sea scallops. *66 Wellington St. W.* ☎ *416/364-0054.*

Restaurant Row

While busier Bloor a block north mostly makes do with generic Thai and Japanese, the small stretch of Harbord Street between Spadina and Bathurst has quickly grown into the city's latest foodie paradise. **Splendido** (p 112) is the strip's pricey pioneer and, despite chef David Lee's decampment, it remains king. Much-admired newcomers the **Harbord Room** (p 108), **Loire** (119 Harbord St.; ☎ 416/850-8330), and **Tati** (124 Harbord St.; ☎ 416/ 962-8284) have packed rooms most nights, serving a wide range of sophisticated, locally grown bistro cuisine. Tati's owners have even opened up their own French cheese shop, **Chabichou** (196 Borden St.; ☎ 647/430-4942), a block west. Finally, for delightful pastries and high-end ice cream, you can't go wrong with sunny **Dessert Trends Patisserie-Bistro** (154 Harbord St.; ☎ 416/916-8155).

Reservations recommended. Entrees $38–$44. AE, DC, MC, V. Lunch & dinner Mon–Fri. Subway: St. Andrew. Map p 102.

★ **C5** YORKVILLE *FUSION* It's one thing to gaze upon the ROM Crystal, it's another thing to eat inside it. But the food will definitely distract you from the view and the decor. The menu's designed to capture Toronto's eclectic culinary landscape and several seafood dishes speak of Asian and Mediterranean influences. *100 Queen's Park.* ☎ *416/586-7928. Reservations recommended. Entrees $25–$36. AE, MC, V. Lunch Tues–Sat, dinner Thurs–Sat. Subway: Museum. Map p 101.*

★ **Colborne Lane** DOWNTOWN *FUSION* Chef Claudio Aprile is the city's foremost practitioner of molecular gastronomy. He opened this, his first restaurant, a few years ago and it's become a popular destination for savvy diners looking for the latest in culinary innovation—from deconstructed ceviche to tea-smoked squab. *45 Colborne St.*

Colborne Lane is celebrated for its culinary innovation.

☎ 416/368-9009. Reservations recommended. Entrees $12–$36. AE, MC, V. Lunch Mon–Fri, dinner Mon–Sun. Subway: King. Map p 102.

Conviction KING WEST *BISTRO* Bad-boy chef Marc Thuet's renowned space at King and Portland has gone through many incarnations. The latest: a restaurant entirely staffed by rehabilitated ex-cons. The prices aren't that criminal, however, and the Mediterranean-inspired food is up to Thuet's exacting standards. *609 King St. W.* ☎ *416/603-2777. Reservations recommended. Entrees $17–$34. AE, MC, V. Dinner Tues–Sat, brunch Sun. Subway: St. Andrew, then 504 King streetcar west. Map p 102.*

Delux WEST QUEEN WEST *FUSION* Occasionally snooty service is more than made up for by this bistro's well-priced Cuban-French food. Where else will you find a pressed Cubano sandwich stuffed with pork, cornichons and Gruyère or frites with chipotle mayo? *92 Ossington Ave.* ☎ *416/537-0134. Entrees $19–$23. AE, MC, V. Dinner Tues–Sat. Subway: Ossington, then 63 Ossington bus south. Map p 102.*

★ **The Drake** WEST QUEEN WEST *BISTRO* Like the see-and-be-seen hotel in which it's housed, this retro dining room blends both the traditional and the cutting edge. High-end, remixed comfort food (made largely with local, seasonal ingredients) is a staple; the mac 'n' cheese and barbecue dishes are popular. *1150 Queen St. W.* ☎ *416/531-5042. Entrees $17–$33. AE, DC, MC, V. Dinner daily, brunch Sun. Subway: Osgoode, then 501 streetcar west. Map p 102.*

E-pan CHINATOWN *CHINESE* With decor more subtle and quaint than the bright, bustling Chinatown joints that surround it, E-pan is a kind of oasis. The food's top-notch and, given the size of the menus, there's a lot of it. The hot-and-sour soup and the scallops are safe bets, but let the servers recommend dishes. *369 Spadina Ave.* ☎ *416/260-9988. AE, MC, V. Lunch & dinner daily. Subway: Spadina, then 510 streetcar south. Map p 102.*

★★ **Foxley** DUNDAS WEST *FUSION* This narrow hot spot brings together two unique things—the fiery pan-Asian cuisine of chef Tom Thai, served tapas style, and the Portuguese neighborhood where his newish restaurant resides. Come for the ceviche, but, given the no-reservations policy, prepare yourself for a possible line at the door. *207 Ossington Ave.* ☎ *416/ 534-8520. Entrees $16–$21. AE, MC, V. Dinner daily Mon–Sat. Subway: Ossington, then 63 Ossington bus south. Map p 102.*

★ **Frank** QUEEN WEST *BISTRO* This elegant restaurant was named for Frank Gehry, the architect who designed both the restaurant and the popular addition to the Art Gallery of Ontario that houses it. This solipsism doesn't extend to the

The Drake serves high-end, remixed comfort food.

satisfying menu, thankfully, which sticks to local ingredients and an all-Ontario wine list. *317 Dundas St. W.* ☎ *416/979-6688. Reservations recommended. Entrees $22–$30. AE, MC, V. Lunch Tues–Fri, dinner Tues– Sun, brunch Sat–Sun. Subway: St. Patrick. Map p 102.*

★ **kids** **Fresh** WEST QUEEN WEST *VEGETARIAN* This member of a 10-year-old local chain of veggie restaurants produces impressive

Fresh boasts affordable, swiftly served vegetarian cuisine.

salads, filling rice, noodle bowls, and excellent fruit smoothies—all for ridiculously low prices. It's usually very busy, but the service and turnover is speedy. *894 Queen St. W.* ☎ *416/553-9923. Entrees $6–$14. MC, V. Lunch & dinner daily. Subway: Osgoode, then 501 streetcar west. Map p 102.*

Fressen QUEEN WEST *VEGETARIAN* While the reasonably priced food can take a while—it's all created from scratch—and can sometimes be bland when it arrives, this is the city's foremost vegan restaurant. Carnivores can indulge in the "fish and chips" (deep-fried tempeh and taro). *478 Queen St. W.* ☎ *416/504-5127. Small plates $9. AE, MC, V. Dinner daily, brunch Sat–Sun. Subway: Osgoode, then 501 streetcar west. Map p 102.*

★★ Gardiner Café YORKVILLE *CAFE* Chef Jamie Kennedy's the king of fresh-and-local cuisine but the recent economic malaise hit him hard. He's scaled back or sold off most of his miniempire and this, his most attractive restaurant, has been condensed to a sandwich-and-salad cafe with an after-work tasting series. But the food is still to die for. *Gardiner Museum, 111 Queen's Park.* ☎ *416/362-1957. Entrees $5–$10. MC, V. Lunch daily. Subway: Museum. Map p 101.*

★★ Grace LITTLE ITALY *BISTRO* This is a serene and sunny place in which to enjoy a pleasing array of simply prepared but very satisfying dishes. Classic Southern U.S. fare is a specialty but fresh, local ingredients get the star turn. The patio's one of the city's best. *503 College St.* ☎ *416/944-8884. Reservations recommended. Entrees $16–$30. AE, MC, V. Dinner Mon–Sat. Subway: Queen's Park, then 506 streetcar west. Map p 101.*

The Harbord Room ANNEX *BISTRO* This is a small room with a small menu, but both are packed with surprises. Tapas-size dishes, like salt cod fritters, rub elbows with more conventional cuisine, from local leg of lamb to a fairly unique Caesar salad. Open 'til midnight on Friday and Saturday, giving other restaurant chefs a place to unwind. *89 Harbord St.* ☎ *416/962-8989. Reservations recommended. Entrees $14–$26. AE, MC, V. Dinner daily, brunch Sun. Subway: Spadina. Walk 2 blocks south, turn right at Harbord. Map p 101.*

★ Indus Junction QUEEN WEST *INDIAN* While lovers of traditional Indian cuisine should head to the east side of town (p 33), this stylish, romantic spot serves as a very respectable substitute. Familiar dishes (shrimp vindaloo, lamb korma) are given a modern spin and the cocktails—definitely try the Mumbai Mango—are a real hit. *811 Queen St. W.* ☎ *416/362-1957. Entrees $11–$15. AE, MC, V. Dinner Tues–Sun. Subway: Osgoode, then 501 streetcar west. Map p 102.*

★★ kids Japango DOWNTOWN *JAPANESE* Tucked behind City Hall, the size of this intimate eatery belies the grandeur of the food. The fish is shockingly fresh, the dishes perfectly authentic. Even the tempura is expertly prepared: light, delicate, and grease free. *122 Elizabeth St.* ☎ *416/599-5557. Entrees $15–$40. MC, V. Lunch & dinner Mon–Sat. Subway: Dundas. Map p 102.*

★★★ Kaiseki-Sakura DOWNTOWN *JAPANESE* A refreshing antidote to the bargain-basement Japanese/Korean joints that plague the city. This is as traditional and as nuanced as it gets. The *omakase* tasting menu, which can feature unique sashimi and the eel-like hora fish, comes in various sizes and prices. Unusual sake pairings accompany each course. *556 Church St.* ☎ *416/923-1010. Tasting menu $80–$120. AE, MC, V. Dinner Wed–Mon. Subway: Wellesley. Map p 102.*

Ki DOWNTOWN *JAPANESE* This place is big and boisterous and a popular after-work spot with the captains of industry that fill the nearby financial towers. The food—a fairly standard, modern Japanese slate—is competent but not life changing. You'll have more fun sticking with the cutely named cocktails (Hello Kitty, anyone?). *181 Bay St.* ☎ *416/308-5888. Entrees $15–$40. AE, DC, MC, V. Lunch Mon–Fri, dinner Mon–Sat. Subway: King. Map p 102.*

★★ **Lai Wah Heen** DOWNTOWN *CHINESE* Offering what's considered the finest Chinese food in the downtown core (the burbs claim even better spots), this tranquil hotel restaurant serves up delectable dim sum every day at lunch and carefully prepared and unique, if

expensive, dinner dishes. *Metropolitan Hotel, 108 Chestnut St.* ☎ *416/977-9899. Entrees $18–$30. AE, DC, MC, V. Lunch & dinner daily. Subway: St. Patrick. Map p 102.*

Madeline's ENTERTAINMENT DISTRICT *FUSION* Susur Lee was once the city's top toque but in 2008 left to open his first New York restaurant. His eponymous eatery, which he still owns, was renamed (after his mother) and gussied up in a "Byzantine" style. The European-style food was simplified, however, and while still excellent, not the revelation Susur was. *601 King St. W.* ☎ *416/603-2205. Reservations recommended. Entrees $18–$25. AE, DC, MC, V. Dinner Mon–Sat. Subway: St. Andrew, then 504 King streetcar west. Map p 102.*

★ **kids Magic Oven** ANNEX *ITALIAN* This local pizza and pasta chain produces beautiful, handmade pies packed with fresh, organic, and unique ingredients (including, yes, a gold leaf garnish). While pricey, it's

Ki is a popular after-work spot for Japanese food.

Magic Oven produces handmade pizzas with unique, organic ingredients.

one of the few places that offers gluten-free crusts and lactose-free cheeses. *270 Dupont St.* ☎ *416/868-6836. Entrees $8–$18. MC, V. Lunch & dinner daily. Subway: Dupont. Map p 101.*

★★ **Mistura** YORKVILLE *ITALIAN* While it's enjoying a newish, somewhat more lavish look, Mistura's rustic Northern Italian food hasn't changed a bit. The emphasis is on traditional preparation and fresh-and-local ingredients. The beet risotto and the pine nut tart are perennial faves. *265 Davenport Rd.* ☎ *416/515-0009. Reservations recommended. Entrees $18–$54. AE, DC, MC, V. Dinner Mon–Sat. Subway: Bay. Map p 101.*

★ kids **Nataraj** ANNEX *INDIAN* This Annex institution turns out consistently solid tandoori dishes and some of the city's best *saag paneer*. The food's rich, though, so count on an early night or afternoon nap. A cheap, extensive, all-you-can-eat buffet lunch attracts local students and profs. *394 Bloor St. W.* ☎ *416/928-2925. Entrees $6–$13. AE, DC, MC, V. Lunch Mon–Fri, dinner daily. Subway: Spadina. Map p 101.*

★★ **Nota Bene** QUEEN WEST *BISTRO* Nestled between the financial district and the funky wilds of Queen West, this nifty spot turns out classy dishes that appeal to both demographics. Chef David Lee made his very renowned mark at Splendido (p 112) but here the emphasis is on simpler, more affordable local fare. A special pretheater menu is available from 5 to 6:30pm on Four Seasons Centre performance days. *180 Queen St. W.* ☎ *416/977-6400. Reservations recommended. Entrees $19–$89. AE, DC, MC, V. Lunch Mon–Fri, dinner Mon–Sat. Subway: Osgoode. Map p 102.*

★ **Oddfellows** WEST QUEEN WEST *BISTRO* This eccentric eatery, owned and operated by the local design firm Castor, is both a showcase for their furnishings and a fun place for dinner. A single communal table is the only seating and the small, French-and-Asian-influenced menu is both inviting and surprising. *936 Queen St. W.* ☎ *416/534-5244. Entrees $12–$39. AE, MC, V. Dinner Mon–Sat, brunch Sat–Sun. Subway: Osgoode, then 501 streetcar west. Map p 102.*

★ **One** YORKVILLE *FUSION* If you can afford it, superstar chef Mark McEwan's latest venture is the place to sit and watch the passing film festival parade. If the fest's not on, however, it's a pretty safe bet you'll still catch some A-lister midcanoodle. Oh, and the food—a wide range of premium seafood and meat dishes designed for sharing—is pretty good too. *116 Yorkville Ave.* ☎ *416/961-9600. Reservations recommended. Entrees $18–$65. AE, DC, MC, V. Lunch & dinner daily. Subway: Bay. Map p 101.*

Oyster Boy WEST QUEEN WEST *SEAFOOD* There are a number of good oyster bars scattered around the city, but this one's the most laid-back and fun. "Mollusks for the masses" is the eatery's motto and they come fresh, with a slew of condiments, or in six different baked varieties. *872 Queen St. W.* ☎ *416/534-3432. Entrees $15–$30. AE, MC, V. Dinner daily. Subway: Osgoode, then 501 streetcar west. Map p 102.*

Superstar chef Mark McEwan's One is popular with celebrities.

The Rosebud QUEEN WEST *BISTRO* A haute cuisine outpost on one of the more colorful blocks of Queen West, this quaint bistro produces consistently fine French classics like well-priced frogs legs and toothsome braised short ribs.

The Rosebud serves classic French bistro dishes.

The Italian Terroni is famous for its eccentric rules.

669 Queen St. W. ☎ *416/703-8810. Reservations recommended. Entrees $24–$32. AE, MC, V. Dinner Tues– Sun. Subway: Osgoode, then 501 streetcar west. Map p 102.*

★ **Salad King** DOWNTOWN *THAI* As insanely busy as this joint can be—usually filled with students from nearby Ryerson University— this is a terrific place for fast, flavorful, and inexpensive Thai. If you don't want to rub elbows with your fellow diners, head upstairs to sister spot, Linda, for a more formal meal. *335 Yonge St.* ☎ *416/971-7041. Entrees $7.75–$9.95. MC, V. Lunch & dinner Mon–Sat. Subway: Dundas. Map p 102.*

★★★ **Splendido** ANNEX *FUSION* Hands down, this is considered the city's most luxurious dining experience. Service is impeccable and the food unique, with the adventurous tasting menus, often containing dishes with a blend of cross-Canada ingredients, the way to go.

88 Harbord St. ☎ *416/929-7788. Reservations recommended. Entrees $46–$65, tasting menu starts at $140. AE, DC, MC, V. Dinner Tues– Sat. Subway: Spadina. Map p 101.*

★★ **kids Terroni** DOWNTOWN *ITALIAN* When the flagship of this immensely popular minichain expanded into bigger, swankier digs, it didn't mean the lunchtime line got any smaller. Nor did it diminish the quality of its traditional pizzas, salads, and pastas. The place is famous for its eccentric rules: no Diet Coke, no substitutions, and absolutely no parmesan on seafood dishes. *57A Adelaide St. E.* ☎ *416/203-3093. Entrees $13–$17. AE, DC, MC, V. Lunch & dinner Mon– Sat. Subway: King. Map p 102.*

★ **Torito** KENSINGTON MARKET *SPANISH* Small plates were a brief craze in Toronto but traditional tapas joints never quite took root. This cute, crowded spot is the exception, however, and it's always hopping. The patio's great in the summer but the downstairs lounge, Pepe's, is a more authentic experience. The smoked trout and new potatoes is perfect. *276 Augusta Ave.* ☎ *416/961-7373. Tapas $3–$12. AE, MC, V. Dinner daily. Subway: Queen's Park, then 506 streetcar west to Augusta. Map p 102.*

kids Utopia LITTLE ITALY *LIGHT FARE* Barring fast-food, this casual spot is where you'll find the neighborhood's cheapest, most filling meal. Consequently, it's almost impossible to get a table (although in summer, the back patio triples capacity). The large menu is packed with burritos, burgers, sandwiches, and salads. *586 College St.* ☎ *416/ 534-7751. Lunch & dinner daily. Subway: Queen's Park, then 506 streetcar west. Map p 101.* ●

Nightlife Best Bets

Best Bar for Friendly Service
★★ Crooked Star, *202 Ossington Ave. (p 120)*

Best Place for a Bachelorette Party
★ El Convento Rico, *750 College St. (p 126)*

Best Classic Cocktails
★★★ The Paddock, *178 Bathurst St. (p 122)*

Best Martini
★ Library Bar, *100 Front St. W. (p 122)*

Best View
★★ Roof Lounge, Park Hyatt Hotel, *4 Avenue Rd. (p 123)*

Best Bar for Meeting Artists
★★ The Ossington, *61 Ossington Ave. (p 122)*

Best Place for a First Date
★ Souz Dal, *636 College St. (p 124)*

Best Bar to Watch the Leafs Play
Philthy McNasty's, *276 King St. W. (p 122)*

Best Beer Selection
★ Beerbistro, *18 King St. E. (p 119)*

Best Jukebox
★★ Sweaty Betty's, *13 Ossington Ave. (p 124)*

Best Place to Spot a Celebrity
★ Drake Hotel, *1150 Queen St. W. (p 146)*

Best Dive Bar
★ Collision, *573 College St. (p 120)*

Best Dance Club
★★ Circa, *126 John St. (p 124)*

Best Gay Bar
★★★ Hair of the Dog, *425 Church St. (p 126)*

Best Irish Pub
★★★ Dora Keogh, *141 Danforth Ave. (p 121)*

Best Spot for Karaoke
★★ Gladstone Hotel, *1214 Queen St. W. (p 121)*

The Drake Hotel attracts crowds of all kinds, including many celebrities.

Previous page: Circa was created by New York nightlife legend Peter Gatien.

Downtown Nightlife

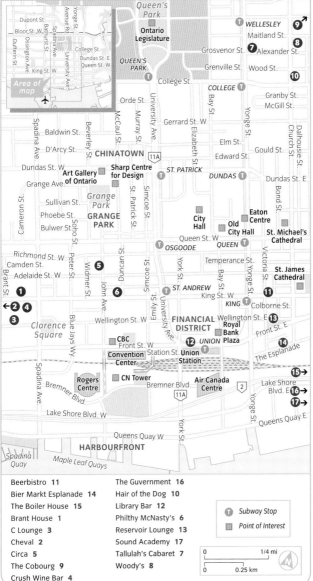

Beerbistro **11**

Bier Markt Esplanade **14**

The Boiler House **15**

Brant House **1**

C Lounge **3**

Cheval **2**

Circa **5**

The Cobourg **9**

Crush Wine Bar **4**

The Guvernment **16**

Hair of the Dog **10**

Library Bar **12**

Philthy McNasty's **6**

Reservoir Lounge **13**

Sound Academy **17**

Tallulah's Cabaret **7**

Woody's **8**

🅣 Subway Stop

▪ Point of Interest

0		1/4 mi
0	0.25 km	

Queen West & Midtown

Nightlife

Toronto Nightlife A to Z

The all-white back patio at Amber.

Bars & Pubs

★ **Amber** YORKVILLE A restaurant/ lounge fit for a club king, the all-white, cabana-like back patio of this club—usually taken over by the beautiful people in the summer—feels like it's been transplanted from Miami. *119 Yorkville Ave. ☎ 416/926-9037. www.amberinyorkville.com. Subway: Bay. Map p 116.*

★★ **Andy Poolhall** LITTLE ITALY This cozy basement pool parlor doubles as a relaxed nightclub. The name's a bad pun on Andy Warhol—it's sister bar, Ciao Edie, is up the street—but the comfy,

Cozy Andy Poolhall doubles as a nightclub.

1960s-style decor and dim lighting are good for canoodling and casual conversation. *480 College St. ☎ 416/923-5300. www.andypoolhall.com. Subway: Queen's Park, then 506 streetcar west. Map p 116.*

Avenue Bar and Lounge YORKVILLE The main-floor bar at the back of the Four Seasons Hotel is just what you'd expect—posh and polished, with expert service, serene ambience, and power brokers sipping strong martinis. *21 Avenue Rd. ☎ 416/928-7332. Subway: Bay. Map p 116.*

★★ **Bar Italia** LITTLE ITALY A College Street nightlife pioneer, this 20-year-old institution remains a neighborhood favorite. Wine is the specialty of the house—there are only four beers on tap—with about 20 reds and 13 whites available. The second-floor bar is only open on Friday and Saturday and is often used for events. *582 College St. ☎ 416/535-3621. www.bar-italia.ca. Subway: Queen's Park, then 506 streetcar west. Map p 116.*

★★ **The Beaconsfield** WEST QUEEN WEST A well-appointed alternative to the Drake, this restaurant/bar is luxurious, warm, and, usually, surprisingly attitude free. Formerly a bank, there's a certain

Algonquin Round Table vibe to the place, though the scenesters at the bar are usually discussing recording contracts rather than poetry manuscripts. *1154 Queen St. W.* ☎ *416/516-2550. www.thebeaconsfield.com. Subway: Osgoode, then 501 streetcar west. Map p 116.*

Bedford Academy YORKVILLE There are 18 beers on tap at this spacious watering-hole, a haunt of Univerity of Toronto grad students and local professionals. Unless it's crowded and loud with conversation, the constant blare of TVs gives it a sports-bar feel. *36 Prince Arthur Ave.* ☎ *416/921-4600. www.the bedfordacademy.com. Subway: Museum. Map p 116.*

★ **Beerbistro** DOWNTOWN Savvy servers know all there is to know about the 120 different beers served here, arranged on the menu by taste—from smoky to fruity. Chocolate beers are a new fave, and the mussels are good too. *18 King St. E.* ☎ *416/861-9872. www.beerbistro. com. Subway: King. Map p 115.*

Bier Markt Esplanade DOWNTOWN Good luck finding a spot on the patio here on a summer Friday afternoon. Inside, however, the cavernous size makes it a favorite for office parties. The Belgian-heavy beer menu is comparably large, with about 100 brews from 25 countries available—the classic frites make for an excellent accompaniment. *58 The Esplanade.* ☎ *416/862-7575. www.thebiermarkt.com. Subway: Union. Map p 115.*

Black Bull Tavern QUEEN WEST As soon as spring has sprung, the sprawling patio (with seating for around 200) fills up with a startling mix of art students, suburban cool hunters, and aging bikers. But stay outside if you can—the drab, dim interior's nothing remarkable. Beer selection is basic. *298 Queen St. W.* ☎ *416/593-2766. www.blackbull.ca. Subway: Osgoode. Map p 116.*

★ **The Boiler House** DISTILLERY This cavernous gastro-pub is housed in one of the Distillery's clutch of converted industrial buildings and its decor includes a 6.7m (22-ft.) wine rack and handmade timber tables. It offers 20 wines by the glass and, of course, a large range of Mill Street beers (from the neighboring brewery). The cobblestone patio's lovely in summer. *55 Mill St., Bldg. 46.* ☎ *416/203-2121. www.boilerhouse.ca.*

Beerbistro serves more than a hundred different brews.

Subway: Castle Frank, then 65A Parliament St. bus south to Mill St. Map p 115.

Bovine Sex Club QUEEN WEST The name's racier than the reality—this Queen West stalwart is really just a sleazy, loud rocker bar. It's been so for about 18 years and the distinctive, intimidating decor—like a Robert Rauschenberg collage thrown on the ceiling—hasn't changed at all in that time. *542 Queen St. W. ☎ 416/504-4239. www.bovinesexclub.com. Subway: Osgoode. Map p 116.*

★★ Brant House ENTERTAINMENT DISTRICT   This lounge-cum-nightclub, a converted Victorian warehouse, is the epitome of the sophisticated King West scene—beautiful, moneyed people (ad execs, film types) bumping, grinding, schmoozing. Early in the evening, cocktails and food are served at communal tables that later disappear once the dancing begins. *522 King St. W. ☎ 416/703-2800. www.branthouse.com. Subway: St. Andrew, then 504 King streetcar west. Map p 115.*

The Brunswick House ANNEX The Brunny is a notorious beer hall where many an undergrad has

developed a taste for cheap draft while dancing to Top 40 tunes. Recent renovations haven't diminished the Animal House luster. *481 Bloor St. W. ☎ 416/964-2242. Subway: Spadina. Map p 116.*

★★ The Cobourg CABBAGETOWN A badly needed shot of sophistication on the Parliament strip, this simple, elegant bar's as comfy as your own living room. (The Peter Doig painting on one wall gives the place its name.) A minimal menu complements a good range of wine and scotch. *533 Parliament St. ☎ 416/913-7538. Subway: Castle Frank, then 65A Parliament St. south. Map p 115.*

★ Collision LITTLE ITALY   People still call this grungy, noisy college mainstay "Ted's," after its previous owner. As the strip's nightlife becomes more clubby and suburban, this dive's lack of pretension, cheap pints, and bargain-basement pool table become more refreshing. *573 College St. ☎ 416/530-7569. Subway: Queen's Park, then 506 streetcar west. Map p 116.*

★★ Crooked Star WEST QUEEN WEST   One of the pioneers of the still-hot Ossington strip, this is possibly the friendliest bar in town. It's

Irish pub Dora Keogh is as authentic as they come.

pretty basic, though—cramped rec-room chic, a small selection of draft, and Tex-Mex nibbles. A Coronation Street brunch is served to hungover regulars every Sunday at 1pm. *202 Ossington Ave.* ☎ *416/536-7271. Subway: Ossington, then 63 Ossington bus south. Map p 116.*

Crush Wine Bar ENTERTAIN-MENT DISTRICT As you'd expect, this attractive restaurant/bar is all about the vino. The menu includes 250 different bottles, 30 to 35 available by the glass. There's even a Center for Wine Affairs, which hosts tastings and classes. *455 King St. W.* ☎ *416/599-7000. www.crushwine bar.com. Subway: St. Andrew, then 504 King streetcar west. Map p 115.*

★★★ Dora Keogh DANFORTH There are many faux Irish pubs in town, but the short stools, copper-top tables, and roaring fire of this authentic gem will transport you to Dublin in a second. The Guinness, of course, is poured just right. *141 Danforth Ave.* ☎ *416/778-1804. www.allens.to. Subway: Broadview. Map p 116.*

★ Drake Hotel WEST QUEEN WEST There are many places to enjoy a drink at this hipster hangout—from the long sidewalk patio to the serene Sky Lounge and the basement Underground, scene of many an intimate rock show. Each spot has a different vibe but you can guarantee your fellow imbibers will be well coiffed, well dressed, and well connected. *1150 Queen St. W.* ☎ *416/531-5042. www.thedrakehotel.ca. Subway: Osgoode, then 501 streetcar west. Map p 116.*

★★ Gladstone Hotel WEST QUEEN WEST Like the Drake, this somewhat hipper (and somewhat grittier) boutique hotel offers multiple spots to wet your whistle. Karaoke's a staple at the legendary Melody Bar and the Gladstone

The Drake Hotel features several different areas to drink, each with a different vibe.

Ballroom, all wood and high ceilings, is a splendid room in which to enjoy a cocktail while taking in a show or book launch. *1214 Queen St. W.* ☎ *416/531-4635. www.gladstone hotel.com. Subway: Osgoode, then 501 streetcar west. Map p 116.*

Hemingway's YORKVILLE The namesake of this multilevel restaurant/pub was briefly a *Toronto Star* reporter in the 1920s and it's easy to imagine Ernest hanging out here today. Far less pretentious and pricey than the bars and restaurants that surround it, it's a good, laid-back place to grab a beer or partake of the extensive wine list. *142 Cumberland St.* ☎ *416/968-2828. www. hemingways.to. Subway: Bay. Map p 116.*

★ Il Gatto Nero LITTLE ITALY The giant TV indicates what a popular place this is to watch soccer, but there's much more to this classy bar and cafe. The coffee's good, the service attentive, and the wine well chosen. The long sidewalk patio is prime people-watching real estate. *720 College St.* ☎ *416/536-3132. www.ilgattonero.ca. Subway: Queen's Park, then 506 streetcar west. Map p 116.*

The Best Nightlife

The Paddock is a classic, timeless bar first opened in 1947.

★ **Library Bar** DOWNTOWN This quaint, quiet bar, housed in the Royal York Hotel, feels like a private club. Or, yes, a library. There are books galore, drinks named after famous writers, and enormous, expensive martinis are a specialty. *100 Front St. W.* ☎ *416/368-2511. www.fairmont.com. Subway: Union. Map p 115.*

Madison Avenue Pub ANNEX Situated on a pleasant, tree-lined avenue dotted with frat houses, this massive, multilevel sports bar is, naturally, a popular haunt for frat boys and the women who love them. A meat market maybe, but in the daytime, it's a convivial lunch spot frequented by professors and other Annexites. *14 Madison Ave.* ☎ *416/927-1722. www.madison avenuepub.com. Subway: Spadina. Map p 116.*

★★ **The Ossington** WEST QUEEN WEST Bigger than your average Ossington hot spot, this has quickly become the most popular new kid on the block. It's dark and moody, generally filled with indie kids and art students—the owners and bartenders are artists themselves—and carries a precisely curated selection

of beer and wine. *61 Ossington Ave.* ☎ *416/850-0161. Subway: Ossington, then 63 Ossington bus south. Map p 116.*

★★★ **The Paddock** QUEEN WEST This classy, dark gin joint, all wood and burgundy leather, has an almost timeless quality to it. No surprise that it opened in 1947 and that Sinatra supposedly drank here. The spot's popular with gimlet-swilling arts professionals and recent renovations have diminished none of the charm. *178 Bathurst St. (at Queen).* ☎ *416/504-9997. www.thepaddock. ca. Subway: Osgoode, then 501 streetcar west. Map p 116.*

Philthy McNasty's ENTERTAINMENT DISTRICT This subterranean bar and grill (formerly a Peel Pub) is part of an Ontario-wide franchise and is your quintessential sports bar. Lots of TVs, fried food, and dudes in hockey jerseys. A good place to watch the game. *276 King St. W.* ☎ *416/979-8060. www. philthymcnastys.com. Subway: St. Andrew. Map p 115.*

Remy's YORKVILLE This staid restaurant has seemingly been around forever and its strongest selling point is still the 300-seat rooftop patio. Skip the standard food, order a beer, and keep your eyes peeled for wandering starlets below. *115 Yorkville Ave.* ☎ *416/968-9429. Subway: Bay. Map p 116.*

Reposado WEST QUEEN WEST Drink fads come and go, but this narrow, grown-up bar is counting on tequila being around for a while. *Good* tequila that is—32 premium brands are available here, at various price points. Unique, Mexican-influenced tapas take the edge off. *136 Ossington Ave.* ☎ *416/532-6474. www.reposadobar.com. Subway: Ossington, then 63 Ossington bus south. Map p 116.*

Reservoir Lounge DOWNTOWN
Notable for its 6-nights-a-week live jazz and blues performances, this 100-seat venue serves up decent *mojitos* and even better crab cakes. The bar likes to trumpet the celebs that have dropped by (Tom Jones, Rod Stewart) but beware the suburban high rollers on weekends. *52 Wellington St. E.* ☎ *416/955-0887. www.reservoirlounge.com. Subway: King. Map p 115.*

★★ Roof Lounge YORKVILLE
With a stunning view (the ROM Crystal has never looked better), this diminutive 18th-floor bar at the top of the Hyatt has long been one of the city's most elegant saloons. While the writers who once hung out here are in short supply today, you'll still find well-heeled publishers and editors rubbing elbows with lawyers and hotel guests. *Park Hyatt Hotel, 4 Avenue Rd.* ☎ *416/324-1568. Subway: Museum. Map p 116.*

Sneaky Dee's LITTLE ITALY
Local wags long ago dubbed this Tex-Mex dive "Sneaky Disease," and you still might want to avoid the nachos (which are served until 4:30am). But the beer's cheap and plentiful and the indie rock and club kids that hang out here are colorful.

The Roof Lounge at the Park Hyatt hotel is one of the city's most elegant bars.

Loads of music acts—from the Barenaked Ladies to Broken Social Scene—have played the small stage. *431 College St.* ☎ *416/603-3090. www.sneaky-dees.com. Subway: Queen's Park, then 506 streetcar west. Map p 116.*

★ The Social WEST QUEEN WEST
With a wall adorned with the artwork *Welfare Allegory for the Death of Parkdale (As We Know It)* and the thrift-store furnishings, this large, industrial space might seem to be thumbing its nose at the Drake down the street. But it's actually

Reposado is the place to go for quality tequila.

Hip Sweaty Betty's is renowned for its excellent jukebox.

filled with as many scenesters and attracts its own share of celebs—Johnny Knoxville and M.I.A. have been known to drop by for beers by the fireplace. *1100 Queen St. W.* ☎ *416/5323-4474. www.thesocial. ca. Subway: Osgoode, then 501 streetcar west. Map p 116.*

★ **Souz Dal** LITTLE ITALY One of the city's more romantic *boîtes,* this adorable hideaway specializes in unique martinis and margaritas. Mixed drinks, as well as Soho and Jolly Rancher martinis, are on special all night Sunday, Monday, and Tuesday. *636 College St.* ☎ *416/537-1883. www.souzdal.com. Subway: Queen's Park, then 506 streetcar west. Map p 116.*

★★ **Sweaty Betty's** WEST QUEEN WEST It's not much bigger than many living rooms, but this hip Ossington outpost was an early harbinger of the strip's happening night life. The excellent jukebox is stocked with everything from Motorhead to Willie Nelson. No table service. Don't even ask. *13 Ossington Ave.* ☎ *416/535-6861. Subway: Ossington, then 63 Ossington bus south. Map p 116.*

Dance Clubs

★ **The Boat** KENSINGTON MARKET It looks like a ship (there are portholes for windows), feels like a ship (especially once you get some $4 beers into you), and, at times, smells like a ship. But the indie kids love it. Depending on the night, the music (and styles) range from '80s disco to '60s doo-wop. *158 Augusta Ave.* ☎ *416/593-9218. Subway: St. Patrick, then 505 Dundas streetcar west to Augusta. Map p 116.*

★ **Cheval** ENTERTAINMENT DISTRICT This discreet club—once upon a time the building housed Royal Canadian Mounted Police horses, hence the use of saddles in the decor—is barely noticeable in the day. But the long lines beginning around 11pm on weekends attest to its popularity. The crowd's full of iPhone-toting lawyers and ad execs and martinis are the drink of choice. *606 King St. W.* ☎ *416/363-4933. www.chevalbar.com. Subway: St. Andrew. Map p 115.*

★★ **Circa** ENTERTAINMENT DISTRICT Nightlife legend Peter Gatien—best known for New York's Limelight—is the mastermind behind this much-hyped 4,924sq.-m (53,000-sq.-ft.) monster club. At that size, there's something for everyone—from a movie theater to a room dedicated to

The Boat night club is designed to look like the inside of a ship.

The massive Circa has everything from a movie theater to a bar in the bathroom.

Kidrobot, the ultracool toy maker. There's even a bar in the bathroom. *126 John St.* ☎ *416/979-0044. www. circatoronto.com. Subway: Osgoode. Map p 115.*

C Lounge ENTERTAINMENT DISTRICT   Skip the spa and head straight to this sensual club, with its indoor waterfalls, reflecting pool, and in-house Aveda masseuses. The music ranges from dance and house to R&B and Top 40. *456 Wellington St. W.* ☎ *416/260-9393. www.liberty group.com. Subway: St. Andrew. Map p 115.*

The Dance Cave ANNEX   This grotty space above concert venue Lee's Palace attracts a youngish crowd, eager to dance to suburban alternative-rebel anthems (from the Violent Femmes to Franz Ferdinand). *529 Bloor St. W.* ☎ *416/532-1598. www.leespalace.com. Subway: Bathurst. Map p 116.*

The Guvernment HARBOUR-FRONT   It's been around for about 20 years, under a variety of names and guises, but this enormous, 2,044sq.-m (22,000-sq.-ft.) club continues to pack them in. With several dance floors and two patios, the crowd's extremely diverse, from glow stick–waving 20-somethings to aging hipsters who still harbor crushes for Moby. *132 Queens Quay E.* ☎ *416/ 869-0045. www.theguvernment.com. Subway: Union. Map p 115.*

★ **The Mod Club** LITTLE ITALY Owner and DJ Mark Holmes might be best known to some as the front man of the '80s rocker band Platinum Blonde, but this midsize nightclub is a testament to his English roots. The tunes tend to the Britpop that's popular with the 20- and 30-something crowd, and the walls are decorated with icons like Mary Quant. The sound system rocks. *722 College St.* ☎ *416/588-4663. www. themodclub.com. Subway: Queen's Park, then 506 streetcar west. Map p 116.*

Sound Academy HARBOUR-FRONT   This far-flung, newly renovated dance club is in the big-ticket, big-crowd, beach-friendly European mold. Cover charges and drink prices are high but the DJs are prestigious—everyone from Tiesto to Fatboy Slim have spun here. *11 Polson St.* ☎ *416/469-5655. www. sound-academy.com. Subway: Union, then 72A Pape east to Polson St. Map p 115.*

The Beaver attracts a younger gay crowd.

Gay and Lesbian Bars and Clubs

★ The Beaver WEST QUEEN

WEST This modest, romantic diner is the requisite hangout for the westward-moving younger queer crowd. The tiny DJ booth can produce surprisingly big sound in the later hours, drowning out the pre-club drinkers and comfort-food snackers. *1192 Queen St. W.* ☎ *416/537-2768. www.beavertoronto.com. Subway: Osgoode, then 501 streetcar west. Map p 116.*

★ El Convento Rico LITTLE ITALY

This queer Latin nightclub, given to playing salsa, meringue, and disco, is legendary for its drag shows and enthusiastic crowds. The non-threatening ambience also attracts legions of women just looking to shake their booties free of lecherous eyes. *750 College St.* ☎ *416/588-7800. www.elconvento*

El Convento Rico is famous for its drag shows and bachlorette parties.

rico.com. *Subway: Queen's Park, then 506 streetcar west. Map p 116.*

★★★ Hair of the Dog DOWN-

TOWN The best local in the gay village, this laid-back and welcoming bar attracts a crowd of all persuasions. They come for the trippy music, stellar wine list, and good nibblies. *425 Church St.* ☎ *416/964-2708. www.hairofthedogpub.ca. Subway: College. Map p 115.*

★ Stones Place WEST QUEEN

WEST This dark, labyrinthine bar is owned by a Rolling Stones fanatic—hence the name and the decor—but it's nonetheless become the site of many popular gay-themed nights. The dance floor gets sweaty. *1255 Queen St. W.* ☎ *416/536-4242. www.stonesplace.ca. Subway: Osgoode, then 501 streetcar west. Map p 116.*

Tallulah's Cabaret DOWNTOWN

By day and early evening this is the Buddies in Bad Times Theatre. On weekend nights, it's transformed into a hip and happening dance floor, where young gays and lesbians gather for cheap drinks and good times. *12 Alexander St. (at Yonge).* ☎ *416/975-8555. www.artsexy.ca. Subway: College. Map p 115.*

Woody's DOWNTOWN This

enormous bar—actually five bars in one—is a Church Street institution. It's appeared in the Showtime drama, *Queer As Folk* and is just as famous for its contests devoted to male body parts and drag shows. *467 Church St.* ☎ *416/972-0887. www.woodys toronto.com. Subway: Wellesley. Map p 115.* ●

A&E Best Bets

Best Jazz Club
★★ The Rex Hotel Jazz & Blues Bar, *194 Queen St. W. (p 135)*

Best Movie Theater for Obscure French Films
★★★ Cinematheque Ontario, *317 Dundas St. W. (p 134)*

Best Hipster Hoedown
★★ The Dakota Tavern, *249 Ossington Ave. (p 137)*

Best Place for a Concert Under the Stars
Molson Amphitheatre, *909 Lakeshore Blvd. (p 138)*

Best Free Classical Music
★★★ Four Seasons Centre for the Performing Arts, *145 Queen St. W (p 25)*

Best Place to Spot a Rising Comic
★★ The Rivoli, *332 Queen St. W. (p 133)*

Best Place for New Canadian Plays
★ Factory Theatre, *125 Bathurst St. (p 139)*

Best Place to Learn New Dance Moves
★ Lula Lounge, *1585 Dundas St. W. (p 135)*

Best Place to Meet a Nobel Prize Winner
★ Authors at Harbourfront, *235 Queens Quay W. (p 136)*

Best Place to Discover New Electronic Music
★★ The Music Gallery, *197 John St. (p 138)*

Best Place to Watch a Documentary
★★ NFB Mediatheque, *150 John St. (p 134)*

Best Place to Watch an Exciting Dance Troupe
★★ Toronto Dance Theatre, *80 Winchester St. (p 134)*

Most Comfy Movie Theater Seats
★ The Royal, *608 College St. (p 135)*

Best Place to Pretend You're on Broadway
★ Princess of Wales Theatre, *300 King St. (p 140)*

Innovative works are performed at the Toronto Dance Theatre.

Previous page: The National Ballet of Canada dances regularly at the Four Seasons Centre for the Performing Arts.

Downtown A&E

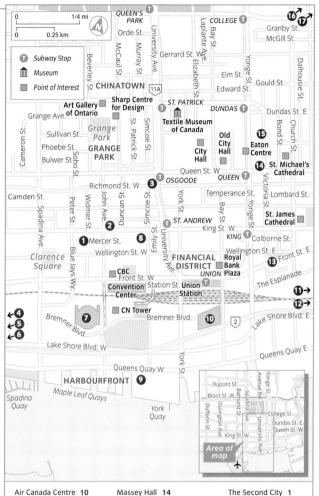

Queen West & Midtown A&E

Cinematheque Ontario **11**
The Dakota Tavern **4**
Factory Theatre **7**
Four Seasons Centre for
  the Performing Arts **15**
The Horseshoe Tavern **10**
Lula Lounge **5**
The Music Gallery **12**
National Film Board
  Mediatheque **14**

The Rex Hotel Jazz &
  Blues Bar **13**
The Rivoli **9**
The Royal **3**
Tafelmusik **2**
Theatre Passe Muraille **8**
This Is Not a
  Reading Series **6**
The Trane Studio **1**

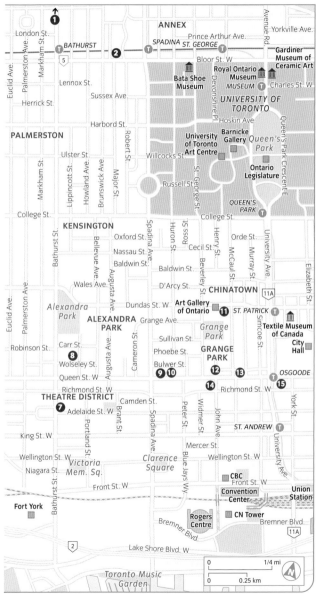

London St.

Markham St.

Palmerston Ave.

Euclid Ave.

1

ANNEX

BATHURST

5

2

SPADINA

Prince Arthur Ave.

ST. GEORGE

Yorkville Ave.

Avenue Rd.

Bloor St. W

Gardiner
Museum of
Ceramic Art

Lennox St.

Sussex Ave.

Bata Shoe
Museum

Royal Ontario
Museum

Charles St. W

MUSEUM

Devonshire Pl.

PALMERSTON

Herrick St.

Harbord St.

*UNIVERSITY OF
TORONTO*

Hoskin Ave.

Ulster St.

University
of Toronto
Art Centre

Barnicke
Gallery

*Queen's
Park*

Markham St.

Lippincott St.

Howland Ave.

Brunswick Ave.

Major St.

Robert St.

Willcocks St.

St. George St.

Ontario
Legislature

Queen's Park Crescent E

Russell St.

*QUEEN'S
PARK*

College St.

College St.

KENSINGTON

Spadina Ave.

Huron St.

St. George St.

Henry St.

Orde St.

University Ave.

Bathurst St.

Bellevue Ave.

Augusta Ave.

Oxford St.

Nassau St.

Baldwin St.

Cecil St.

McCaul St.

Murray St.

Elizabeth St.

Baldwin St.

D'Arcy St.

Beverley St.

CHINATOWN

11A

Euclid Ave.

Palmerston Ave.

Wales Ave.

Dundas St. W

Art Gallery
of Ontario

11

ST. PATRICK

*Alexandra
Park*

**ALEXANDRA
PARK**

Grange Ave.

*Grange
Park*

Simcoe St.

Textile Museum
of Canada

City
Hall

Robinson St.

Carr St.

Sullivan St.

**GRANGE
PARK**

Cameron St.

Phoebe St.

12

13

Wolseley St.

8

Augusta Ave.

Bulwer St.

9 **10**

14

OSGOODE

15

Queen St. W

Richmond St. W

Richmond St. W

THEATRE DISTRICT

7

Camden St.

Adelaide St. W

York St.

King St. W

Portland St.

Brant St.

Spadina Ave.

Peter St.

Widmer St.

John Ave.

ST. ANDREW

Wellington St. W

Niagara St.

*Victoria
Mem. Sq.*

Mercer St.

*Clarence
Square*

Blue Jays Wy.

Wellington St. W

University Ave.

Front St. W

CBC

Front St. W

Union
Station

Fort York

Bathurst St.

Convention
Center

CN Tower

Bremner Blvd.

Rogers
Centre

Bremner Blvd.

11A

2

Lake Shore Blvd. W

0   1/4 mi

0   0.25 km

*Toronto Music
Garden*

Toronto A&E A to Z

The Toronto Symphony Orchestra gives regular concerts at Roy Thomson Hall.

Classical and Opera

★★★ Four Seasons Centre for the Performing Arts QUEEN
WEST   Toronto's long-awaited dedicated opera house opened in 2006. Since then, the hall has seen a steady stream of spectacular productions, from the Michael Levine–designed *Ring Cycle* to James Kudelka's much-beloved *Nutcracker*. *See p 25,* **6**. *Map p 130.*

Tafelmusik is one of the world's leading baroque orchestras.

★ Roy Thomson Hall ENTERTAINMENT DISTRICT   This Arthur Erickson–designed concert hall opened in 1982 and is the permanent home of the Toronto Symphony Orchestra as well as occasional host to big-name pop and classical acts. During the Toronto International Film Festival, celebs and paparazzi take over. *60 Simcoe St.* ☎ *416/593-4822. www. roythomson.com. Tickets $45–$195. Subway: St. Andrew. Map p 129.*

★ St. Lawrence Centre for the Arts DOWNTOWN   This performing arts stalwart—housing the Bluma Appel and Jane Mallet theatres—recently enjoyed a $3-million makeover and its reinvigorated spaces are now even better showcases for theatrical works by the Canadian Stage Company and various opera and music ensembles. *27 Front St. E.* ☎ *416/366-7723. www. stlc.com. Tickets $15–$58. Subway: Union. Map p 129.*

★★ Tafelmusik ANNEX   One of the world's finest baroque orchestras—a recent American tour culminated with a stop at Carnegie

Hall—this 19-member ensemble performs works by Handel, Bach, and more on genuine period instruments. Their usual home is the charming Trinity-St. Paul's United Church, but larger concerts are held at the George Weston Recital Hall (5040 Yonge St.) and Massey Hall (178 Victoria St.). *427 Bloor St. W.* ☎ *416/964-6337. www.tafelmusik. org. Tickets $15–$79. Subway: Spadina. Map p 130.*

Comedy
★★ The Rivoli QUEEN WEST Birthplace of the notorious Kids in the Hall, this funky Queen West landmark continues to host pee-your-pants-funny comedy. The ALT-dotCOMedy Lounge kicks off every Monday at 9pm (get there early, there's only 125 seats) while every Tuesday night, the Sketch Comedy Lounge showcases a revolving set of troupes. *332 Queen St. W. (at Spadina).* ☎ *416/596-1908. www. rivoli.ca. Tickets PWYC. Subway: Osgoode. Map p 130.*

★ The Second City ENTERTAINMENT DISTRICT While Second City may have its roots in Chicago, many of the improv club's legends—everyone from John Candy to Martin Short—got their start at this Canuck outpost. The main stage's specialty is pun-heavy, provocative political revues. *51 Mercer St.* ☎ *416/343-0011. Tickets $23–$28, dinner packages available. Subway: Union. Map p 129.*

Yuk Yuk's ENTERTAINMENT DISTRICT Thirty years old and now the world's largest chain of comedy clubs, Mark Breslin brainchild got its start right here (more specifically, down at Harbourfront). Pro comics are featured Wednesday through Sunday, with an Amateur Night on Tuesday (including aspirants from nearby Humber College). Reservations are preferred. *224 Richmond St. W. (at University).* ☎ *416/967-6425. www.yukyuks. com. Tickets vary depending on night, dinner package available. Subway: Osgoode. Map p 129.*

Dance
★ Dancemakers DISTILLERY This 30-year-old company has had some of the country's foremost dancers among its number,

The Second City comedy club has produced international stars like John Candy and Martin Short.

The Toronto Dance Theatre is home to the city's pre-eminent contemporary dance troupe.

including Robert Desrosiers and Peggy Baker. It set up a permanent home in the Distillery in 2002, giving birth to the Dancemakers Centre for Creation, which holds master classes, choreographic labs, and occasional lectures. *55 Mill St., Bldg. 74.* ☎ *416/367-1800. www.dance makers.org. Tickets $18–$38. Subway: Castle Frank (from there, take the 65A Parliament St. bus south to Front, walk 2 blocks south to Mill St.). Map p 129.*

★★ Toronto Dance Theatre

CABBAGETOWN   Led by legendary choreographer Christopher House, this contemporary dance troupe is dedicated to the creation of original works that range from collaborations with pop bands like the Hidden Cameras to innovative fusions of dance with science, film, and philosophy. Wannabes can attend a Saturday morning company class for $8. *80 Winchester St.* ☎ *416/967-1365. www.tdt.org. Ticket prices vary. Subway: Castle Frank (from there, take the 65 Parliament St. bus south to Winchester, about a 5-min. ride). Map p 129.*

Film

★★★ Cinematheque Ontario

QUEEN WEST   Mecca for the film-geek crowd, this is the city's preeminent showcase for obscure foreign fare, Hollywood classics, and film festival hits too marginal for mainstream theaters. The quietest audiences in town. *Jackman Hall, Art Gallery of Ontario, 317 Dundas St. W.* ☎ *416/968-3456. www.cinema thequeontario.ca. Tickets $5.90–$12. Subway: St. Patrick. Map p 130.*

Cinesphere HARBOURFRONT

There are a few places to watch IMAX movies in Toronto—the Science Centre, the Scotiabank Theatre—but this is the biggest and best. *See p 39,* **10**. *Map p 129.*

★★ kids National Film Board Mediatheque QUEEN WEST

Curl up in one of the private screening booths and, for only two bucks, you have fingertip access to over 5,000 of the board's award-winning documentaries and animated films. *150 John St.* ☎ *416/973-3012. www.nfb.ca/mediatheque. Tickets*

Movie Madness

For 10 days every September, the red carpets are rolled out for the world's second-largest film fest, the **Toronto International Film Festival** (www.tiff.net). Around 300 films from over 50 countries are shown, with Hollywood boldfaces happily swarming over the city, posing for pix, and scooping up swag. But this is just the splashiest such event. All year long, just about every week, Toronto is host to at least one other major film fest or another, including the experimental and avant-garde **Images Festival** (www.images festival.com) and the **Toronto Jewish Film Festival** (www.tjff. com) in April; North America's largest documentary showcase, **Hot Docs** (www.hotdocs.ca) and the gay and lesbian fest, **Inside Out** (www.insideout.on.ca) in May; and the **Reel Asian International Film Festival** (www.reelasian.com) in November.

$2/all day, free for children 11 and under. Subway: Osgoode. Map p 130.

★ **The Royal** LITTLE ITALY   Of the city's remaining repertory theaters—there are about half a dozen—this Art Deco gem is both the comfiest and, in terms of programming, the most exciting. Several small film fests (see "Movie Madness," above) are held here, as well as screenings of first- and second-run indie flicks. *608 College St.* ☎ *416/534-5252. Tickets $8–$10. Subway: Queen's Park (take the 506 College streetcar west to Clinton). Map p 130.*

Jazz and Cabaret

★ **Lula Lounge** DUNDAS WEST   A beacon in Little Brazil (a largely desolate section of Dundas that's just now gentrifying), this nightclub specializes in salsa, meringue, and an eclectic fusion of African, Cuban, and Brazilian music. Weekends feature special dance and dinner packages ($54 per person), with lessons for left-footed newbies. *1585 Dundas St. W.* ☎ *416/588-0307. www. lulalounge.ca. Cover varies. Subway: Dufferin (from there, take the 29*

Dufferin bus south to Dundas, then walk 5 min. west). Map p 130.

★★ **The Rex Hotel Jazz & Blues Bar** QUEEN WEST   The Rex has morphed from shabby dive bar to the city's preeminent jazz destination. (Okay, it's retained a bit of the shabbiness.) With about 1,000 shows a year, the intimate club attracts a steady stream of major jazz and

Lula Lounge has dance lessons and concerts by Latin and African musicians.

This Is Not a Reading Series asks authors to present their work in unconventional ways.

blues players, from Wynton Marsalis to Maceo Parker. On Tuesday, different house bands host the Classic Rex Jazz Jam, where the stage is open to anyone eager to show off their chops. *194 Queen St. W. ☎ 416/598-2475. www.therex.ca. Cover $6–$9 for some shows. Subway: Osgoode. Map p 130.*

The Trane Studio ANNEX This beautiful little room is only 5 years old but it's already established itself as one of the city's coolest spots for jazz. (The name says it all, of course, a tip of the hat to sax player John Coltrane.) There's more than jazz on tap, though, everything from dub poetry nights to CD release parties. A full menu's available. *964 Bathurst St. ☎ 416/913-8198. Cover varies. Subway: Bathurst. Map p 130.*

Literary

★ **Authors at Harbourfront Centre** HARBOURFRONT Name a writer and he or she has been here. The granddaddy of the city's lit events, this respected weekly series (held Sept–June) has hosted more than 5,000 authors over the last 35

years, including 15 Nobel laureates. In October, this is the site of the prestigious International Festival of Authors and, in May, its junior edition, ALOUD: A Celebration for Young Readers. *235 Queens Quay W. ☎ 416/973-4600. www.readings.org. $8. Subway: Union (take either the 509 Exhibition or 510 Spadina streetcar from Union to Lower Simcoe St.). Map p 129.*

★★ **This Is Not a Reading Series** WEST QUEEN WEST Fed up with the usual author appearance where the writer stands on stage, reads from book, and signs books for fans? Pages bookstore launched this alternative series 5 years ago. Now you can see writers—everyone from Kathleen Turner to Neal Stephenson—talk about their books, play the banjo, show films, or play with puppets. Schedules vary but there's generally one or two events a week throughout the year. *Gladstone Hotel, 1214 Queen St. W. ☎ 416/598-1447. $5. Subway: Osgoode (from there, take the 501 streetcar west to Queen and Gladstone). Map p 130.*

Cheap Thrills

Attending pro sports events can be an expensive proposition, but there are other, much-less-expensive ways, to enjoy some spirited competition. The non-NHL **Toronto Maple Leafs** are part of the Intercounty Baseball League and play free games from May through July in Christie Pits (750 Bloor St., at Christie St.; www.theibl.ca). The **University of Toronto (U of T) Varsity Blues** football team isn't exactly known for its stellar play (its been known to lose 49 games in a row) but the team's new stadium is cheap ($10 per person if you're not a U of T student) and convenient (Varsity Centre, 299 Bloor St. W.; ☎ 416/946-7201; www.varsityblues.ca). The **Toronto Marlies** (Ricoh Coliseum, 100 Princes' Blvd.; www.torontomarlies.com), who play hockey in the Ricoh Coliseum, are the Leafs' farm team and have a better record than their pricey pro counterparts. Tickets range from $10 to $38.

Pop and Rock

★★ The Dakota Tavern WEST QUEEN WEST Descend the stairs to this hip honky-tonk and you'll feel like you've been transported to Nashville around 1978. Live boot-scootin' boogie—everything from country to bluegrass—is served up here every night of the week. The tunes usually get started around 9pm, with the dancing picking up soon after. *249 Ossington Ave. ☎ 416/850-4579. www.thedakotatavern.com. Cover varies. Subway: Ossington (from there, take the 63 Ossington bus south to Dundas). Map p 130.*

★ Horseshoe Tavern QUEEN WEST Slightly spiffed up with new tiles and tables, the city's most venerable saloon—now 60 years old—is still hopping. Every local act has cut its teeth here and bands like the Rolling Stones routinely hold secret, surprise shows. Every Tuesday, DJ Dave "Bookie" Bookman's famed Nu Music Nite highlights undiscovered talent. *370 Queen St. W. ☎ 416/598-4753. www.horseshoetavern.com. Cover varies. Subway: Osgoode. Map p 130.*

★★★ Massey Hall DOWNTOWN Over 110 years old, this legendary Victorian auditorium has been graced by everyone from the Dalai Lama to Morrissey. (Gordon Lightfoot's returned the most frequently, traditionally playing a show every spring since 1967.) The acoustics are amazing but the seating can be

The legendary stage at the Horseshoe Tavern.

The venerable Massey Hall has been hosting top performances for over a century.

cramped. *178 Victoria St.* ☎ *416/ 872-4255. www.masseyhall.com. Ticket prices vary. Subway: Queen. Map p 129.*

Molson Amphitheatre HAR-BOURFRONT *The* place for a summertime concert, this lakeside venue brings in a wide variety of big-name pop acts. Assigned seating is available but first-come, first-served lawn seating makes for a more memorable experience. Your ticket also gets you admission to the Ontario Place amusement park. *909 Lakeshore Blvd.* ☎ *416/260-5600. www.ontario place.com. Ticket prices vary. Subway: Bathurst (from there, take Bathurst streetcar south to Exhibition Place, last stop). Map p 129.*

★★ The Music Gallery QUEEN WEST Toronto's intriguing "center for creative music," this nonprofit space is home to new and experimental music of all stripes, especially free jazz and avant-rock. Its location in St. George the Martyr Church (at the edge of Grange Park) lends every concert a particularly hallowed feel. *197 John St.* ☎ *416/ 204-1080. www.musicgallery.org. Ticket prices vary. Subway: St. Patrick. Map p 130.*

The Phoenix Concert Theatre CABBAGETOWN While it may be one of the city's less-charming venues, this nightclub is also one of the most popular. The draw is its size— 1,672sq. m (18,000 sq. ft.) with a balcony lounge (Le Loft) that overlooks the main room. Despite the lack of ambience, the cavernous spot hosts an eclectic range of acts from Hot Chip to Johnny Winter. *410 Sherbourne St.* ☎ *416/323-1251. www. libertygroup.com. Ticket prices vary. Subway: Sherbourne. Map p 129.*

Sports

Air Canada Centre DOWNTOWN Once upon a time, this was the old Canada Post Building and artifacts from the original post office can be glimpsed in the Air Canada Centre galleria. But this 10-year-old, state-of-the-art arena is now much better known as the hangar-shaped home of the Maple Leafs and Raptors, the city's pro hockey and basketball teams. Big-name entertainers—the Madonnas and Springsteens of the world—also hold regular concerts here, with the acoustic quality dependent on the configuration of seating arrangements. *40 Bay St.*

☎ 416/815-5500. www.theaircanada centre.com. Ticket prices vary. Subway: Union. Map p 129.

★ **BMO Field** HARBOURFRONT
The city's latest, hottest sports team—sorry, Leafs fans—is its soccer club, Toronto FC, the first Major League Soccer outfit outside of the U.S. (Tickets are extremely hard to come by and there are waiting lists for season seat packages.) BMO Field is likewise the first soccer-specific stadium in the country and is home both to Toronto FC and the Canadian national team. The fans' infectious enthusiasm for the sport makes for some very boisterous games. *170 Princes Blvd.* ☎ *416/360-4625. www.bmofield.com. Tickets $21–$220. Subway: Bathurst (from there, take the 511 streetcar to Exhibition Place). Map p 129.*

Rogers Centre DOWNTOWN
The stadium formerly known as the SkyDome is still home to major league baseball's Toronto Blue Jays, the CFL's Toronto Argonauts and the world's first fully retractable roof. (It can open or close in 20 min.) In the off season, the sportsplex is used for concerts, the annual Canadian Aboriginal Festival, monster truck rallies, and Disney on Ice. *1 Blue Jays Way.* ☎ *416/341-1000. www.rogers centre.com. Ticket prices vary. Subway: Union (from there, follow the SkyWalk west). Map p 129.*

Theater

Canon Theatre DOWNTOWN
Over the course of its nearly 100 years of operation, this opulent Thomas Lamb–designed building has morphed from live theater to movie multiplex and back again. Beginning life as the Pantages Theatre, it became the Pantages again in 1989, most famous for being the home of *The Phantom of the Opera*. Today, the Canon's in the hands of

the Mirvish family, who has done much to revitalize big-budget musical theater in Toronto, and has presented such diverse shows as *Spring Awakening* and *The Color Purple*. *244 Victoria St.* ☎ *416/872-1212. www.mirvish.com. Tickets $50–$99. Subway: Dundas. Map p 129.*

★ **Factory Theatre** QUEEN WEST
The first company to dedicate itself entirely to new Canadian plays (by definition, a daring proposition), the 38-year-old Factory is actually two theatrical spaces in one. The main stage seats 200 and the tiny studio theater is used for more experimental works. Some of the company's most renowned productions include several of George Walker's edgy plays as well as work by Jason Sherman and Claudia Dey. *125 Bathurst St. (at Adelaide).* ☎ *416/504-9971. www.factorytheatre.ca. Tickets $10–$37. Subway: Bathurst (from there, take the 511 Bathurst streetcar south to Adelaide). Map p 130.*

Major League Soccer's TFC enjoys the support of boisterous crowds at BMO Field.

The Princess of Wales Theatre hosts blockbuster productions like The Lord of the Rings *and* The Sound of Music.

★ Princess of Wales Theatre

ENTERTAINMENT DISTRICT   Mirvish Productions built this 2,000-seat, state-of-the-art playhouse in 1993 to properly present its lavish, helicopter-starring production of *Miss Saigon*. (The Mirvish family also owns the historic, neighboring Royal Alexandra Theatre.) It remains home to lavish, mainstream spectacles like *The Lord of the Rings* and *The Sound of Music*. Much of the interior, including the ceiling dome, is covered in murals by artistic *éminence grise* Frank Stella. *300 King St. W.* ☎ *416/872-1212. www.mirvish. com. Tickets $30–$200. Subway: St. Andrew. Map p 129.*

Theatre Passe Muraille QUEEN

WEST   In English, this venerable alternative house's name literally means "theater beyond walls." Born in the late 1960s, its countercultural spirit has been present in provocative plays written by Michael Ondaatje and Linda Griffiths, among many others. The seasons can include up to nine separate productions.

16 Ryerson Ave. ☎ *416/504-7529. www.passemuraille.on.ca. Tickets PWYC–$35. Subway: Osgoode (from there, take the 501 streetcar west to Queen and Ryerson). Map p 130.*

★★ Young Centre for the Performing Arts DISTILLERY   The

product of a partnership between George Brown College's Theatre School and the Soulpepper Theatre Company, this stunning 4,181sq.-m (45,000–sq.-ft.) performance space specializes in classical repertory theater. Notable recent successes have included Tom Stoppard's *Travesties*, *Antigone*, and the experimental *Doing Leonard Cohen*. A 2008 expansion of its mandate means increased mentoring, a new cabaret series, and collaboration with the Luminato Festival. *55 Mill St., Bldg. 49.* ☎ *416/866-8666. www.young centre.ca. Tickets $28–$62. Subway: Castle Frank (from there, take the 65A Parliament St. bus south to Front, walk 2 blocks south to Mill St.). Map p 129.* ●

Lodging Best Bets

Best **Business Hotel**
★★ InterContinental Toronto Yorkville Hotel $$$ *220 Bloor St. W. (p 148)*

Best **Historic Hotel**
★★ Fairmont Royal York $$$$ *100 Front St. W. (p 146)*

Best **Funky Hipster Hotel**
★ The Drake Hotel $$$ *1150 Queen St. W. (p 45)*

Best **Pool**
Sheraton Centre $$ *123 Queen St. W. (p 149)*

Best **for Families**
★ Delta Chelsea $$ *33 Gerrard St. W. (p 145)*

Best **Cheap Bed**
★ Victoria College $ *73 Queen's Park Crescent (p 150)*

Best **Budget Hotel**
Hotel Victoria $ *56 Yonge St. (p 148)*

Most **Romantic Hotel**
★ Windsor Arms $$$ *18 St. Thomas St. (p 150)*

Best **Views**
★ Suites at One King West $$ *1 King St. W. (p 150)*

Best **Hotel Spa**
★★★ Park Hyatt $$$ *4 Avenue Rd. (p 149)*

Best **Boutique Hotel**
★★★ Hotel Le Germain $$$ *30 Mercer St. (p 147)*

Most **Unique Rooms**
★★★ Gladstone Hotel $$ *1214 Queen St. W. (p 146)*

Best **In-House Restaurant**
★ Hazelton Hotel $$$$ *118 Yorkville Ave. (p 147);* and Metropolitan Hotel $$ *108 Chestnut St. (p 148)*

Best **Service**
★★★ Soho Metropolitan Hotel $$$ *318 Wellington St. (p 149)*

Best **High Tea**
★★ Four Seasons $$$$ *21 Avenue Rd. (p 146)*

Best **In-House Bar**
★★★ Park Hyatt $$$ *4 Avenue Rd. (p 149);* and ★★ Fairmont Royal York $$$ *100 Front St. W. (p 146)*

The ballroom inside the historic Fairmont Royal York.

Previous page: An artist-designed room inside the Gladstone Hotel.

Downtown & Waterfront
Lodging

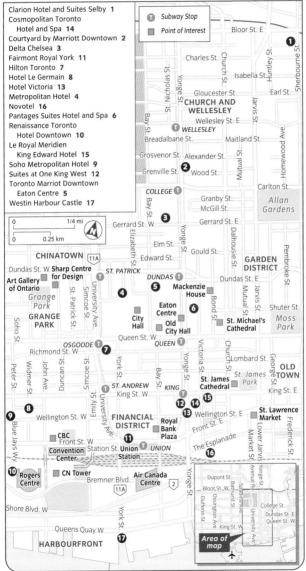

Clarion Hotel and Suites Selby **1**
Cosmopolitan Toronto
    Hotel and Spa **14**
Courtyard by Marriott Downtown **2**
Delta Chelsea **3**
Fairmont Royal York **11**
Hilton Toronto **7**
Hotel Le Germain **8**
Hotel Victoria **13**
Metropolitan Hotel **4**
Novotel **16**
Pantages Suites Hotel and Spa **6**
Renaissance Toronto
    Hotel Downtown **10**
Le Royal Meridien
    King Edward Hotel **15**
Soho Metropolitan Hotel **9**
Suites at One King West **12**
Toronto Marriot Downtown
    Eaton Centre **5**
Westin Harbour Castle **17**

- Subway Stop
- Point of Interest

Queen West & Midtown
Lodging

Casa Loma Inn 1
The Drake Hotel 10
Four Seasons 5
Gladstone Hotel 11
Hazelton Hotel 6

Holiday Inn 2
InterContinental
Toronto Yorkville
Hotel 3
Park Hyatt 4

Sheraton Centre 12
The Sutton Place Hotel 9
Victoria College 8
Windsor Arms 7

Toronto Lodging A to Z

★ **Casa Loma Inn** ANNEX   An adorable Victorian mansion a few blocks south of its namesake tourist attraction, this is a well-priced, well-appointed alternative to bigger hotels. Each room has Internet access, Jacuzzi baths, and a fridge, letting you pretend you're living in the city rather than just visiting. *21 Walmer Rd.* ☎ *416/924-4540. 23 units. Doubles $80. MC, V. Subway: Spadina. Map p 144.*

Clarion Hotel and Suites Selby DOWNTOWN   This historic hotel's biggest claim to fame is that Ernest Hemingway stayed here when he worked for the *Toronto Star* in the 1920s. You'd be forgiven for thinking parts of the hotel haven't changed since then—the rooms aren't fancy and some are a bit shabby. It's affordable, though, centrally located, and very gay friendly. *592 Sherbourne St.* ☎ *800/387-4788. www.hotelselby. com. 82 units. Doubles $105–$160. AE, MC, V. Subway: Sherbourne. Map p 143.*

★ **Cosmopolitan Toronto Hotel and Spa** ENTERTAINMENT DISTRICT This boutique hotel bills itself as "Zen in the city," and while it may not be the meditative experience you'd expect, this is still a serene place to spend a night. The design is sleek, the suites (only five per floor) are catalog-perfect, and they come complete with complimentary incense. *8 Colborne St.* ☎ *800/958-3488. www.cosmotoronto.com. 97 units. Doubles $149–$199. AE, MC, V. Subway: King. Map p 143.*

kids Courtyard By Marriott Downtown DOWNTOWN   While the quality of the rooms is inconsistent (make sure you get one that doesn't face rowdy Yonge St.) the location is superb. Friendly staff and a refurbished gym help too. *475 Yonge St.* ☎ *800/847-5075. 575 units. Doubles $129–$174. AE, DC, MC, V. Subway: College. Map p 143.*

★ **kids Delta Chelsea** DOWNTOWN   This immense, well-located hotel bends over backwards to accommodate kids. The indoor pool features downtown's only water slide, the Kid Centre offers Nintendo games, and Club 33 is a new teen lounge complete with a Ping-Pong

The serene Cosmopolitan Toronto Hotel.

table, iPod docks, and an Xbox 360. Kids 16 and under stay for free if accompanied by an adult. *33 Gerrard St. W. ☎ 800/243-5732. www. deltahotels.com. 1,590 units. Doubles $149–$169. AE, DC, MC, V. Subway: College. Map p 143.*

★ **The Drake Hotel** WEST QUEEN WEST This is the boutique hotel that revolutionized West Queen West. The chic rooms can be tiny (the smallest are called "crash pads") and the bustling hotel itself is a bit far-flung for traditional tourists. But if you're looking for an exceptional experience, this is the place to stay—you'll meet lots of locals and maybe even a celeb or two. *1150 Queen St. W. ☎ 416/531-5042. www. thedrakehotel.ca. 19 units. Doubles $199–$329. AE, MC, V. Subway: Osgoode, then 501 streetcar west. Map p 144.*

★★ **Fairmont Royal York** ENTERTAINMENT DISTRICT In 1929, this gigantic, château-style hotel was the tallest building in the entire British Empire. It was also the first hotel in Canada to have elevators and today it has the largest kitchen and laundry in the country, five restaurants, three rooftop beehives, and, oddly, Toronto's smallest bar, York Station. *100 Front St. W. ☎ 800/441-1414. www. fairmont.com/royalyork. 1,365 units. Doubles $209–$309. AE, DC, MC, V. Subway: Union. Map p 143.*

★★ **Four Seasons** YORKVILLE This is the customary choice for visiting celebs during film festival season and while it's impossible to get a room then, star sightings are easy to come by. Rooms are as luxe as you'd expect—corner suites are best— though many are on the small side. Afternoon tea in the Lobby Bar's a special treat. *21 Avenue Rd. ☎ 416/ 964-0411. www.fourseasons.com. 380 units. Doubles $345–$460. AE, DC, MC, V. Subway: Bay. Map p 144.*

★★★ **Gladstone Hotel** WEST QUEEN WEST The Drake's hipper, less-flashy cousin, this former flophouse asked local artists to design each of its 51 rooms when it was dramatically renovated in 2005. Check out the hotel's website to see which suits your taste—they range widely from Heidi Earnshaw's elegant Sugarbush to Alyson Mitchell's wacky Faux Naturelle, complete with a fun fur wall hanging. *1214 Queen St. W. ☎ 416/531-4635. www.gladstone hotel.com. 51 units. Doubles $185– $475. AE, MC, V. Subway: Osgoode, then 501 streetcar west. Map p 144.*

The indoor pool at the Delta Chelsea hotel.

The Fairmont Royal York was built in 1929.

★ **Hazelton Hotel** YORKVILLE
Giving the Four Seasons a run for its
film-fest money, this newish luxury
hotel is the city's only 5-star hotel.
Accordingly, the spacious rooms
possess a Hollywood glitz: deep
black marble tubs and TVs built into
the mirrors. The 26-seat screening
room is perfect for PowerPoint pre-
sentations or blockbuster previews.
118 Yorkville Ave. ☎ *866/473-6301.
www.thehazeltonhotel.com. 77
units. Doubles $395–$525. AE, DC,
MC, V. Subway: Bay. Map p 144.*

★ **Hilton Toronto** ENTERTAIN-
MENT DISTRICT   As Hiltons go, it
might not be that special or unique,
but this is a solid, comfortable business hotel, just steps from the Financial District. All rooms feature
workstations with high-speed Internet and two telephones with voice
mail. Competitive rates. *145 Richmond St. W.* ☎ *800/445-8667. www.
hilton.com. 600 units. Doubles $129–
$194. AE, DC, MC, V. Subway:
Osgoode. Map p 143.*

Holiday Inn ANNEX   If you don't
plan to send much time in your room,
this middle-of-the-road, midsize hotel
does the job. Rates are surprisingly
good, especially given its proximity to
the University of Toronto, the Annex,

Yorkville, and several museums. *280
Bloor St. W.* ☎ *877/660-8550. www.
holidayinn.com. 209 units. Doubles
$127–$160. AE, MC, V. Subway: St.
George. Map p 143.*

★★★ **Hotel Le Germain** ENTER-
TAINMENT DISTRICT   Part of a Quebec chain of boutique hotels, this is
a little bit of Montreal in Hogtown.
Impeccable design and service and
lots of little perks, from the downstairs lounge/library with complimentary cappuccino to a rooftop
vineyard and putting green. *30 Mercer St.* ☎ *866/345-9501. www.
germaintoronto.com. 122 units.*

*The Hazelton Hotel is a favorite for visit-
ing celebrities during the film festival.*

The historic King Edward Hotel has hosted Elizabeth Taylor and the Beatles.

Doubles $255–$355. AE, DC, MC, V. Subway: St. Andrew. Map p 143.

Hotel Victoria DOWNTOWN
A stately facade belies the largely drab, if clean, interior of this long-lived budget hotel. You'll pay for the enviable location, though, mere steps from the Hockey Hall of Fame and other attractions. *56 Yonge St.* ☎ *800/363-1666. www.hotelvictoria-toronto.com. 56 units. Doubles $95–$159. AE, MC, V. Subway: King. Map p 143.*

★★ **InterContinental Toronto Yorkville Hotel** YORKVILLE This

is another popular spot at film-fest time, with its pool deck often used for interviews. The staff, used to pushy paparazzi, is courteous and accommodating, and the rooms are comfortable and classy—the "executive work desks" are actually large enough to work at. *220 Bloor St. W.* ☎ *877/660-8550. www.ichotelsgroup.com. 208 units. Doubles $149–$485. AE, DC, MC, V. Subway: St. George. Map p 144.*

★ **Le Royal Meridien King Edward Hotel** DOWNTOWN The opulence might have faded a bit, despite many facelifts, but this is still a glamorous place to spend the night. (Everyone from Liz Taylor to the Beatles has.) The rooms are tasteful, though walls can sometimes be thin. *37 King St. E.* ☎ *416/863-9700. www.starwoodhotels.com/lemeridien. 298 units. Doubles $155–$249. AE, DC, MC, V. Subway: King. Map p 143.*

Metropolitan Hotel DOWNTOWN
The best thing about this business hotel—part of a small independent chain—is the excellent dim sum restaurant, Lai Wah Heen, on the second floor. Otherwise, service can be spotty and the rooms, while aspiring to high-end boutique level, are

The European-style Novotel hotel.

sometimes inadequate. A superb, if somewhat hidden, location. *108 Chestnut St.* ☎ *800/668-6600. www. metropolitan.com/toronto. 427 units. Doubles $145–$210. AE, DC, MC, V. Subway: St. Patrick. Map p 143.*

★ **Novotel** ENTERTAINMENT DISTRICT On the quiet, pretty Esplanade, midway between St. Lawrence Market and the Air Canada Centre, this European-style business hotel seems both secluded and in the heart of everything. Parking can be a problem, but Union Station and the TTC are conveniently nearby. *45 The Esplanade.* ☎ *416/367-8900. www.novotel.com. 262 units. Doubles $149–$249. AE, MC, V. Subway: Union. Map p 143.*

★ **Pantages Suites Hotel and Spa** DOWNTOWN If you're looking for the peace and quiet of a Zen monastery with the chic sophistication of a Soho loft, reserve one of the 14 suites on this boutique hotel's Serenity Floor. Each comes with a yoga mat, Jacuzzi tub, and air purifier. Other suites range from 35sq. m to 72sq. m (375–775 sq. ft.) and all feature luxurious linens, designer kitchens, and flatscreen TVs. *200 Victoria St.* ☎ *866/852-1777. www. pantageshotel.com. 229 units. Doubles $129–$179. AE, DC, MC, V. Subway: Queen. Map p 143.*

★★★ **Park Hyatt** YORKVILLE Directly across the street from the Royal Ontario Museum, this is one of the best hotel addresses in town. The luxurious rooms are spacious and the furnishings sumptuous. Stay in the simpler, older tower if you can, although some street noise does leak in. The popular Stillwater Spa downstairs offers perfect pampering. *4 Avenue Rd.* ☎ *416/925-1234. www.parktoronto.hyatt.com. 346 units. Doubles $264–$370. AE, DC, MC, V. Subway: Museum. Map p 144.*

The rooms at the Park Hyatt are spacious and luxurious.

kids **Renaissance Toronto Hotel Downtown** ENTERTAINMENT DISTRICT Located literally inside the Rogers Centre, this is billed as the world's only four-diamond hotel located in a major sports venue. Whether that's a pro or con, depends, perhaps, on your affection for the Blue Jays. Seventy spacious rooms actually overlook the field, so you can watch from the comfort of your own bed. *1 Blue Jays Way* ☎ *800/237-1512. www.marriot.com. 348 units. Doubles $199–$249. AE, DC, MC, V. Subway: Union. Map p 143.*

kids **Sheraton Centre** DOWNTOWN If you're not here for a convention, your best bet is to linger by the pool. The indoor/outdoor Olympic is this monstrous business hotel's best feature. And you can even keep working there, thanks to the Wi-Fi (and seasonal bar). *123 Queen St. W.* ☎ *800/325-3535. www.sheraton toronto.com. 1,377 units. Doubles $190–$260. AE, DC, MC, V. Subway: Osgoode. Map p 144.*

★★★ **Soho Metropolitan Hotel** ENTERTAINMENT DISTRICT Better designed and equipped than its sister hotel on Chestnut Street (p 148), this is a stylish boutique hotel beloved by visiting celebs, athletes, and hipper business folk. For those planning an extended stay, private suites, with regular housekeeping, are available from $3,000 a month. *318 Wellington St.* ☎ *416/599-8800. www.metropolitan.com/soho. 89 units. Doubles $250–$340. AE, DC, MC, V. Subway: St. Andrew. Map p 143.*

★ Suites at One King West

ENTERTAINMENT DISTRICT   With breathtaking views and surprisingly affordable rooms, this is a blend of old (this was once the grand head office of the Dominion Bank) and new Toronto. Located on bustling King Street, however, makes parking tricky. *1 King St. W.* ☎ *866/470-5464. www.onekingwest.com. 500 units. Doubles $129–$229. AE, DC, MC, V. Subway: King. Map p 143.*

The Sutton Place Hotel DOWN-TOWN   An inexplicable favorite with the film-fest crowd, this colossal fortress aspires to European elegance but offers only garden-variety (though reasonably priced) accommodations and an inconvenient location. *955 Bay St.* ☎ *416/924-9221. www.suttonplace.com. 294 units. Doubles $144–$200. AE, DC, MC, V. Subway: Wellesley. Map p 144.*

The rooms at the Windsor Arms are elegant and romantic.

★ Toronto Marriot Downtown Eaton Centre DOWNTOWN

While the Eaton Centre remains an overrated shopping experience, this modish hotel, which connects to the mall, offers exceptional digs. It also boasts unparalleled access to several sightseeing spots. *525 Bay St.* ☎ *800/905-0667. 459 units. Doubles $159–$239. AE, DC, MC, V. Subway: Dundas. Map p 143.*

★ Victoria College BLOOR STREET

If reliving your college days is on your itinerary, these simply furnished, quiet dorm rooms (complete with linens, breakfast, and shared bathrooms) are the place to crash. At any rate, they're the cheapest. Only available in the summer, alas. *73 Queen's Park Crescent.* ☎ *416/585-4524. www.vicu.utoronto.ca. 800 units. Doubles $70–$80 (twin beds only). AE, MC, V. Subway: Museum. Map p 144.*

Westin Harbour Castle HAR-BOURFRONT   Right on the lip of the lake, this mammoth business hotel offers, not surprisingly, some grand views. The rooms can be attractive, as well, but once you're out of the hotel, it's a fairly long walk—under a bleak, crowded expressway—to anything worth seeing up close. *1 Harbour Sq.* ☎ *416/869-1600. www.starwood hotels.com/westin. 977 units. Doubles $150–$175. AE, DC, MC, V. Subway: Union. Map p 143.*

★ Windsor Arms BLOOR STREET

Located on a quiet side street just south of Yorkville, this neo-Gothic building is one of the most attractive small hotels in town. While the rooms can be quite elegant and romantic, there is a gloomy, almost haunted feel to the lobby and bars. *18 St. Thomas St.* ☎ *877/999-2767. www.windsorarmshotel.com. 28 units. Doubles $250–$325. AE, DC, MC, V. Subway: Bay. Map p 144.* ●

Niagara Falls & Niagara-on-the-Lake

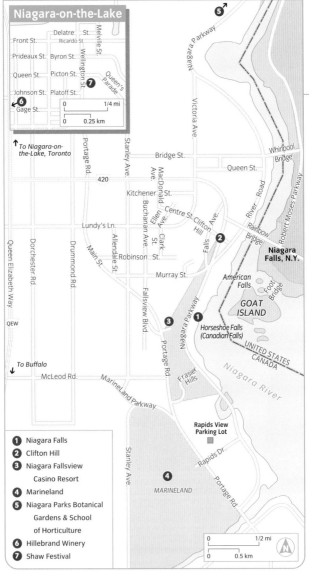

Niagara-on-the-Lake

Delatre St.
Melville St.
Front St. Ricardo St.
Prideaux St. Byron St.
Queen St. Picton St. **7**
Johnson St. Platoff St.
6 Gage St.

Wellington St.

Queen's Parade

0   1/4 mi
0   0.25 km

↑ To Niagara-on-the-Lake, Toronto

5 ↗

Niagara Parkway

Victoria Ave.

Whirlpool Bridge

Bridge St.

Queen St.

Portage Rd.

Stanley Ave.

420

MacDonald Ave.

Kitchener St.

Ellen Ave.

Centre St. Clifton Hill

Falls Ave.

River Road

Robert Moses Parkway

Lundy's Ln.

Buchanan Ave.

Clark St.

2

Rainbow Bridge

Niagara Falls, N.Y.

Allendale St.

Robinson St.

Murray St.

American Falls

Foot Bridge

Queen Elizabeth Way

Dorchester Rd.

Drummond Rd.

Main St.

Fallsview Blvd.

3

Niagara Parkway

1

GOAT ISLAND

Horseshoe Falls (Canadian Falls)

UNITED STATES
CANADA

QEW

↓ To Buffalo

McLeod Rd.

Marineland Parkway

Portage Rd.

Frasier Hills

Niagara River

Rapids View Parking Lot

Stanley Ave.

4

MARINELAND

Rapids Dr.

Portage Rd.

0   1/2 mi
0   0.5 km

1 Niagara Falls
2 Clifton Hill
3 Niagara Fallsview Casino Resort
4 Marineland
5 Niagara Parks Botanical Gardens & School of Horticulture
6 Hillebrand Winery
7 Shaw Festival

Previous page: A Muskoka chair adorned with red maple leafs.

Two hours away from Toronto and one of the most spectacular attractions on the continent, the famous falls are definitely worth a day trip. (If you can, see them in both summer and winter.) The surrounding town, however, isn't quite as majestic, long the clichéd stomping ground of newlyweds, tourists, and—thanks to the three casinos that now serve the area—gamblers. You'll be better off spending some time wandering around Niagara-on-the-Lake, a picturesque town a half-hour away that's home to some of Ontario's finest wineries and the venerable Shaw Festival. START: **Drive or take the train to Niagara Falls (see Practical Matters, below).**

1 ★★★ [kids] **Niagara Falls.**
They're big and beautiful and one of the top tourist destinations in the country. Some quick facts: The falls are roughly 12,000 years old and 55m (180-ft.) high, and 6 million cubic feet (about a million bathtubs worth) flow over the crestline every minute. Conventional wisdom has it that the Canadian side, the so-called Horseshoe Falls, is more attractive (I tend to agree). The best—and most traditional—way to see them is from the ***Maid of the Mist*** (5920 River Rd ; ☎ **905/358-5781**), a boat that takes you right into the falls. You can also get a great view from the slightly pricey **Skylon Tower Observation Deck** (5200 Robinson St.; ☎ **905/356-2561**) or watch the falls' dramatic history in the comfort of the **IMAX Theater** (6170 Buchanan Dr.; ☎ **905/358-3611**). While most visitors flock here in the warmer months, the winter can offer an even more breathtaking experience.

2 [kids] **Clifton Hill.** The main drag of Niagara Falls, a knot of hotels, restaurants, and attractions, is tacky and overpriced, yes, but its seedy charms have been delighting visitors for more than 60 years. Ripley's Believe or Not! Museum (4960 Clifton Hill; ☎ **905/356-2238**) is here, as well as the Movieland Wax Museum of the Stars (4946 Clifton Hill; ☎ **905/358-3676**) and the 18-hole Dinosaur Park minigolf course (4946 Clifton Hill; ☎ **905/358-3293**).

The Maid of the Mist *approaches Horseshoe Falls.*

A blackjack table at Fallsview Casino.

3 Niagara Fallsview Casino Resort. This is the latest gambling emporium to open in Niagara Falls, and also the swankiest. The complex boasts over 3,000 slot machines (almost twice as many as nearby Casino Niagara) and 100 gaming tables. The 1,500-seat theater attracts such big-name dinosaurs as Crosby, Stills & Nash and Huey Lewis. *6380 Fallsview Blvd.* ☎ *888/325-5788.*

4 ★ kids Marineland. Walruses and dolphins and killer whales, oh my! This popular water park is home to numerous aquatic attractions, including the Arctic Cove, three interconnected pools filled with adorable belugas just waiting to be hand fed. Other amusements include a petting zoo and the Sky Screamer, billed as the world's tallest triple tower ride (four times as high as the falls themselves). *7657 Portage Rd.* ☎ *905/356-9565. www.marinelandcanada.com. Admission $40 adults, $33 children 5–9, free for children 4 and under. May 16–June 26 daily 10am–5pm; June 27–Sept 6 daily 9am–6pm; Sept 6–Oct 11 daily 10am–5pm.*

5 ★ kids Niagara Parks Botanical Gardens & School of Horticulture. Just a 10-minute drive away and the perfect antidote to the crass commercialism of the falls, this is 40 hectares (100 acres) of natural beauty. The rose garden alone features 2,400 flowers and

A tour of Hillebrand Winery will let you sample a wide range of the region's offerings.

Practical Matters: Niagara

By car from Toronto, take the Queen Elizabeth Way (QEW) to Niagara-on-the-Lake in the direction of Hamilton and St. Catharines, and exit at Hwy. 55 (about 1½ hr.). Continue south along Niagara Parkway for half an hour to get to the falls. VIA Rail (☎ 888/842-7245; www.viarail.ca) and Amtrak (☎ 800/872-7245; www.amtrak.com) run trains from Toronto and New York, although they stop only in Niagara Falls and St. Catharines, not Niagara-on-the-Lake.

Lodging: Of all the hotel chains with locations in Niagara Falls, the gleaming, well-appointed **Sheraton on the Falls** (5875 Falls Ave., Niagara Falls; ☎ 905/374-4445; doubles $80–$185) ranks first in terms of views (many rooms have balconies). **Abel Thomas House** (259 Regent St., Niagara-on-the-Lake; ☎ 905/468-9625; doubles May–Oct $150–$170, Nov–Apr $125–$145) is a quintessential B&B—lots of floral patterns and antiques—a short walk away from the main drag of Queen Street.

Dining: If you can avoid it, skip the eateries at the falls and head to the upscale ★★★ **Treadwell Cuisine** (61 Lakeport Rd., St. Catharines; ☎ 905/934-9797) in St. Catharines. The farm-to-table menu showcases local produce, often harvested that day, and rare regional wines. For a more casual meal, try the ★★ **Epicurean** (84 Queen St., Niagara-on-the-Lake; ☎ 905/468-3408), a bistro that serves excellent sandwiches and salads on an adorable patio or in its Provençal dining room.

the remarkable Butterfly Conservatory is a habitat for over 2,000 tropical butterflies, all floating freely among lush vegetation. Guided horse-drawn carriage tours of the gardens are conducted throughout the summer. *2565 Niagara Pkwy. Free admission to the gardens; Butterfly Conservatory admission $12 adults, $6.80 children 6–12, free for children 5 and under. Open year-round except Dec. 25.*

❻ ★★ Hillebrand Winery. Niagara Falls boasts 6,070 hectares (15,000 acres) of vineyards and 68 wineries but you can get a good taste of the region's offerings by taking a tour of this celebrated winery restaurant, the area's first. The Winery Experience series includes special meals, tastings, and winemaking

events. *1249 Niagara Stone Rd. ☎ 905/468-7123. www.hillebrand.com. Tours ($10–$99) are available year-round; check the website for the schedule.*

❼ ★ Shaw Festival. Named in honor of the great British dramatist George Bernard Shaw, this esteemed festival, held April through October, performs works by Shaw, contemporaries like Noel Coward, as well as new plays by Canadian writers. The plays are staged in a cluster of different theaters in Niagara-on-the-Lake; check the website for times and venues. Seats can go fast in high season so advance reservations are recommended. ☎ 800/511-7429. www.shawfest.com. Tickets $30–$110.

Muskoka

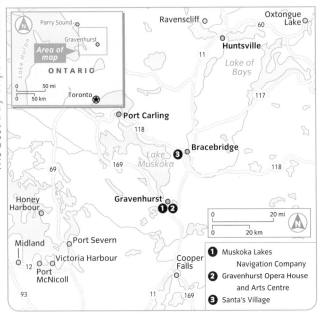

Parry Sound
Gravenhurst
Lake Huron
Area of map
ONTARIO
0   50 mi
0   50 km
Toronto

Ravenscliff
Oxtongue Lake
60
Huntsville
11
Lake of Bays
117
Lake Muskoka
Port Carling
118
Bracebridge ❸
169
118
69
Honey Harbour
Gravenhurst ❶❷
Midland
12
Port Severn
Victoria Harbour
Port McNicoll
93
Cooper Falls
11   169

0   20 mi
0   20 km

❶ Muskoka Lakes Navigation Company
❷ Gravenhurst Opera House and Arts Centre
❸ Santa's Village

In the summer, many Torontonians retreat to their "cottages," seasonal properties that can range from humble cabins to palatial mansions. Thousands of both can be found up in the spectacular Muskoka Lakes, a region known, not surprisingly, as cottage country. Technically, it's a 90-minute drive north of the city, but on a hot July Friday the bumper-to-bumper traffic means you'll be lucky to get there in twice that time. It can be worth the drive, however, to stay at one of the exclusive inns, resorts, or spas that dot the region. The major towns surrounding the lakes—Gravenhurst, Bracebridge, and Huntsville—offer many amenities and attractions. **START: Drive or take the train to Muskoka (see Practical Matters, below).**

❶ ★ **kids** **Muskoka Lakes Navigation Company.** Sailing is one of the region's premier pastimes and there are a variety of ways to enjoy the water. This company's fleet, however, boasts the *Segwun*, North America's oldest operating steamship. Several cruising options are available, depending on how long you want to go out, whether you want a meal onboard, and which parts of the lakes you want to see. The Millionaire's Row cruise glides past a stretch of shoreline famous for its astounding summer homes, many dating back to the 19th century. *185 Cherokee Lane, Gravenhurst.* ☎ *866/687-6667. www.realmuskoka.com. Tickets $29–$83.*

Practical Matters: Muskoka

By car from Toronto, take Hwy. 400 to Hwy. 11. It's about 159km (99 miles) from Toronto to Gravenhurst and then 14km (9 miles) from Gravenhurst to Bracebridge and 80km (50 miles) more to Huntsville. VIA Rail (☎ 888/842-7245; www.viarail.ca) services those towns from Union Station.

Lodging: Deerhurst Resort (1235 Deerhurst Dr., Huntsville; ☎ 800/461-4393; www.deerhurstresort.com; summer doubles $200–$450) is Ontario's largest year-round golf, nature, and spa resort. Popular for conferences, it's also perfect for family vacations. Just as gorgeous, but somewhat more down-home, the **Inn at the Falls** (1 Dominion St., Bracebridge; ☎ 877/645-9212; www.innatthefalls.net; doubles $115–$200) consists of seven Victorian houses that overlook the Muskoka River.

Dining: With a name like ★★★ **Elements Culinary Theatre** (in the Taboo Resort, 1209 Muskoka Beach Rd., Gravenhurst; ☎ 800/461-0236), you can rightfully expect gastronomic magic. Be advised, though, the six-course fusion (Japanese-European) tasting menu is the only option available. Every Wednesday in the summer, you can pick up picnic fixings at the **Gravenhurst Farmer's Market** (Muskoka Wharf; www.gravenhurstfarmersmarket.com).

❷ **Gravenhurst Opera House & Arts Centre.** The year-round center of Muskoka cultural life for more than 100 years, this heritage theater hosts comedy, dance, live music, and, on occasion, opera performances. *295 Muskoka Rd. S.* ☎ *705/687-5550. www.gravenhurst.ca.*

❸ **kids Santa's Village.** As odd as it may be for a winter wonderland to be in an area beloved for its warm weather pleasures, this amusement park has been going strong for over 50 years. Eccentric highlights include the Christmas Ball Ferris Wheel, Santa's Splashzone, and a minigolf course called Mister Rudolph's Birdies and Bogeys. More entertainment can be found at Santa's Craft Workshop, a kiddie do-it-yourself depot. *1624 Golden Beach Rd., Bracebridge.* ☎ *705/645-2512. www.santasvillage.ca. Tickets $27*

adults and children 5 and over, $22 seniors and children 2–4, free for children 1 and under 2.

A golfer tees off at Deerhurst Resort.

Stratford

- **1** Shakespeare Gardens
- **2** Chocolate Barr's Candies
- **3** Sputnik Espresso Bar
- **4** Queens Park
- **5** Gallery Stratford
- **6** The Stratford Antique Warehouse
- **7** Shakespeare

Information
Point of Interest
Post Office

Theater lovers should make the two-hour trek to this historic town. It's home to one of North America's finest Shakespeare festivals, an obvious fact given all the local allusions—the Avon River, restaurants named the Old Prune, and so forth. For 50 years, ever since Sir Alec Guinness strode its boards, Stratford has been putting on critically acclaimed productions of plays by the Bard, as well as other classical and contemporary repertoire. There's much more to the town than Shakespeare, however: Fine dining (one of Canada's best cooking schools is also here), antiques, and other arts festivals also enjoy pride of place. START: **Drive or take the train to Stratford (see Practical Matters, below).**

1 ★★ **Shakespeare Gardens.** This classic English garden in the center of town is considered by many to be Stratford's most alluring attraction. It contains flowers named in the plays, a serene lagoon, and a bust of the Bard himself. ⏲ *30 min. Next to Perth County Court House (west end of Ontario St. at Huron).*

2 ★★ kids **Chocolate Barr's Candies.** There are a number of sweet shops in town, but this chocolatier tops them all. A hundred handmade confections are available, from specialty truffles to sponge toffee. Some of the machines producing the candy date from 1909. ⏲ *30 min. 136 Ontario St.* ☎ *519/272-2828.*

The Shakespeare Gardens, located near the Huron Street Bridge.

3 Sputnik Espresso Bar. There's much competition for the pretheater coffee crowd, but this place does a mean macchiato. *46 Ontario St.* ☎ *519/273-6767. $.*

4 kids Queens Park. Stratford has over 46 hectares (115 acres) of formal park land and this large, appealing park represents some of the loveliest. Located just west of the Festival Theatre—one of the Stratford

Festival's premiere venues—it's a great place to stroll and picnic and offers a fine view of the Avon River's famous swans. ⏱ *1 hr.*

5 ★ Gallery Stratford. Dedicated to regional artists and located in the town's historic former pump house, this gallery is full of surprising, often innovative, art. The permanent collection includes over 1,000 works of art and past exhibits

The entrance to the Sputnik Espresso Bar.

The Play's The Thing

Stratford's *raison d'etre* is the annual **Stratford Festival** (April—November), a theatrical extravaganza largely devoted, of course, to Shakespeare's greatest hits. The festival's newish director, the flamboyant and wealthy Des McAnuff, has sought fresh populism and more buzz, although the fare remains much the same: The most recent season included *Hamlet, Cyrano de Bergerac,* and *A Funny Thing Happened on the Way to the Forum.* Many well-known Canadian actors appear here, so if you have a hankering for Paul Gross or Colm Feore (a Stratford regular), get your tickets. A bevy of other related events—backstage tours, lectures, post-performance discussions—also regularly take place. For information and tickets call ☎ **800/567-1600** or go to www.stratfordfestival.ca.

Practical Matters: Stratford

By car from Toronto, take Hwy. 401 to interchange 278 at Kitchener. Follow Hwy. 8 west onto Hwy. 7/8 to Stratford. The drive's about an hour-and-a-half. The train is easy too (and only just over two hours one-way), especially as Stratford is compact and easy to stroll around. VIA Rail (☎ 888/842-7245; www.viarail.ca) runs trains several times a day along the Toronto-Kitchener-Stratford route.

Lodging: Not necessarily what you'd expect from such a Victorian village, **Xis** (6 Wellington St.; ☎ 519/273-9248; www.xis-stratford.com; doubles $325–$355) is a chic new boutique hotel complete with marble baths and Bulgari toiletries. **Touchstone Manor** (325 St. David St.; ☎ 519/273-5820; www.touchstone-manor.com; doubles $148–$365), meanwhile, is considered Stratford's best B&B, a Georgian Revival mansion a few blocks from downtown.

★★★ Dining: The Old Prune's (151 Albert St.; ☎ 519/271-5052) prices might be high, but the food's worth it. A fairy-tale setting is the backdrop for flawless seafood and meat dishes. For a faster meal, grab a sandwich at the **★ York Street Kitchen** (41 York St.; ☎ 519/273-7041). The James Beard quote on the wall gives you an idea of the quality.

have included photographs by Ed Burtynsky and sculpture by Gareth Lichty. Pathways, dotted with outdoor sculpture, wend through the attractive surrounding parkland. ⏱ *1 hr. 54 Romeo St. S.* ☎ *519/271-5271. Admission $5 adults, $4 seniors and students.*

❻ The Stratford Antique Warehouse. It's not the most picturesque shop, but this massive mall spans 2,043sq.-m (22,000-sq.-ft.), includes 140 different vendors, and is open seven days a week. The collectables for sale vary widely, from Depression-era glass to Star Wars figurines. ⏱ *1 hr. 2977 Forrest Rd.* ☎ *800/259-5116.*

❼ ★ Shakespeare. A 5-minute drive east from Stratford, this quaint hamlet is renowned for its many antiques shops. Many of the dealers, including the high-end **Jonny's Antiques** (*10 Shakespeare St.;*

☎ *519/625-8307*) carry a wide range of Canadiana, furnishings, brass, and porcelain. The 464 sq.-m (5,000-sq.-ft.) **Land & Ross** (*29 Huron Rd.;* ☎ *519/625-8070*) specializes in antique farm furniture and reproductions. ⏱ *2 hr.* ●

Jonny's Antiques in Shakespeare.

The
Savvy Traveler

Before You Go

Government Tourist Offices

In North America: The fastest way to get up-to-date Toronto tourism information is to visit the Tourism Toronto website www.seetoronto now.com or call ☎ 800/499-2514. For information about the rest of Ontario visit www.ontariotravel.net or call ☎ 800/668-2746. Canadian consulates in the U.S. do not provide tourist information.

In the U.K.: The above information is pertinent for British travelers as well, although they can also visit the Canadian High Commission at MacDonald House, 1 Grosvenor Sq., London, W1X 0AB (☎ 0207/258-6600; www.unitedkingdom.gc.ca).

The Best Times to Go

Toronto is great to visit at any time of the year (save, perhaps, dark and frigid Feb), but spring and fall are best. Summers can be very hot and humid and, despite the abundance of festivals and nightlife during the season, many locals retreat to summer homes in the north. The cooler seasons that bookend the summer, however, bring a rich array of cultural activity (especially for film buffs), a reinvigorated populace and cooler temperatures for enjoying a pleasant alfresco lunch or patio cocktail. Nights can still get cool, though—especially with those Lake Ontario breezes—so pack a light jacket.

Festivals & Special Events

SPRING In late March, Toronto eases out of the winter doldrums with **Canada Blooms** (www.canada blooms.com), a flower festival featuring 2.4 hectares (6 acres) of blooming gardens and a convention center full of the latest green-thumb gadgets and products. **Hot Docs**

(www.hotdocs.ca) (late Apr) is North America's largest documentary film festival, featuring almost 200 films from dozens of countries. During May, still-photography buffs swarm hundreds of the city's galleries during **Contact** (www.contactphoto. com), an annual month-long festival of photography with over 1,000 local and international artists. During **Doors Open** (www.toronto.ca/doors open), held over 2 days in late May, 175 buildings of historic, architectural, or cultural significance (many that are normally closed to the general public) open up for free tours.

SUMMER It's hard to pick just a few of the city's dozens of ethnic and cultural festivals—there's one every weekend in the summer. **Luminato** (www.luminato.com), the crown jewel of June, brings together dozens of unusual performances by international artists, musicians, and dancers. The **Pride Week and Pride Parade** (www.pridetoronto. com) celebrates Toronto's gay and lesbian community in late June, culminating with one of the largest parades in North America. **Caribana** (www.caribana.com), (early Aug) is a massive, 42-year-old, 2-week celebration of the city's Caribbean culture, attracting over a million rump-shaking partiers. The bittersweet end of summer is signaled by the mid-August opening of the **Canadian National Exhibition** (www.theex.com), an 18-day pageant of midway rides, cotton candy, agricultural displays, and air shows.

FALL After Labor Day, the city becomes Hollywood North with the opening of the 10-day-long **Toronto International Film Festival** (www.

The previous page: The Harbourfront LRT along Queens Quay Boulevard.

AVERAGE MONTHLY TEMPERATURES & RAINFALL

	JAN	FEB	MAR	APR	MAY	JUNE
High °F/°C	30/-1	31/-1	39/-4	53/12	64/18	75/24
Low °F/°C	18/-8	19/-7	27/-3	38/3	48/9	57/14
Rainfall (in./mm)	1.6/40	1.3/33	3.1/79	3.5/89	4.4/112	3.8/96

	JULY	AUG	SEPT	OCT	NOV	DEC
High °F/°C	80/27	79/26	71/22	59/15	46/8	34/1
Low °F/°C	62/17	61/16	54/12	45/7	35/2	23/-5
Rainfall (in./mm)	4.2/107	4.6/117	3.1/79	2.8/71	2.5/64	2.2/56

tiff.net), the world's second-largest film fest. (Yonge St. was literally shut down a couple years ago because Angelina Jolie showed up—to the organizers' surprise.) The immensely popular **Scotiabank Nuit Blanche** (www.scotiabanknuitblanche.ca), "a free all-night contemporary art thing," transforms the downtown core into a riotous (but usually family-friendly) playground of installation and performance. For more than 30 years, the **International Festival of Authors** (www.readings.org) has brought thousands of Booker and Pulitzer and Giller winners to Harbourfront for its acclaimed 10-day literary festival in October.

WINTER In early December, the **One of a Kind Show** (www.oneofakind show.com) holds its Christmas event (another's held in spring), bringing together over 800 artisans and designers, all selling unique fashions, crafts, and home decor pieces. **WinterCity** (www.toronto. ca/special_events/wintercity) is a city-sponsored, citywide carnival of music, culture, and food, held in late January. Events happen indoors and out, ranging from films at the National Film Board Mediatheque to free concerts at Nathan Philips Square. Winterlicious, probably the most popular program, is a month-long prix-fixe lunch and dinner series that takes over hundreds of city restaurants (it's warm-weather counterpart, Summerlicious, takes

place during July). **Chinese New Year** (www.harbourfrontcentre.com/ www.cccgt.org) celebrations burst out all over the city in early February, from Harbourfront to the northern Chinese Cultural Centre.

The Weather

Toronto's weather can be occasionally extreme (bitter winter lows of -10°C/14°F, highs above 30°C/86°F for a few days in the summer), but much of the year is pleasant and mild. In spring (early Apr to early June) and fall (mid-Sept to early Nov), expect daytime temperatures around 15°C (58°F). Snowfall tends to be relatively moderate and usually only from late December to the end of March. Lake Ontario has a tremendous effect on the city's temperatures, however, and it's usually as much as five degrees cooler by its shores. The lake's the source of the sometimes unbearable summer humidity and, in winter, some streets, especially Bay Street, channel its fierce breezes right through downtown.

Cellphones

GSM (Global System for Mobiles) phones work in Canada, although there are still few Canadian carriers (Rogers, Fido) that employ this system. If you do have a GSM phone, call your wireless operator and ask for international roaming to be activated. Remember, though, that such charges can be surprisingly high

Useful Websites

- **www.toronto.com** Owned by the *Toronto Star* newspaper, this site provides basic info about shopping, events, nightlife, and restaurants.
- **www.torontolife.com** This is the website of the monthly city magazine, *Toronto Life,* complete with a database of its trusted, opinionated restaurant reviews.
- **www.torontoist.com** Now in partnership with the *Globe and Mail* national newspaper, this is a sassy blog about all things Toronto.
- **www.nowtoronto.com** This is the website of *Now,* the city's preeminent free alternative-weekly newspaper. It features up-to-the-minute entertainment listings.
- **www.tourismtoronto.com** Tourism Toronto's official site provides one-stop advice on hotels, attractions, and special deals.
- **www.ttc.ca** The Toronto Transit Commission's official site offers schedules, routes, and maps for the subways, buses, and streetcars and information on fares, passes, and service delays.

unless you're coming from the U.S. and your carrier has an agreement with a Canadian carrier. If you prefer, you can rent a phone while in Toronto from Hello Anywhere (☎ 888/729-4355 in North America; ☎ 800/0729-4355 internationally; www.helloanywhere.com). Several hotels, including the Park Hyatt and the Sutton Place Hotel also offer phones for rent.

Car Rentals
You don't need a car to get around Toronto. In fact, you're better off without one. As in any city its size, traffic downtown is a nightmare (and it's even worse on the highways that crisscross the city). But if you're planning a day trip and want to rent a car for that, all of the major rental companies are represented at the airport and throughout the city. (See Toll-Free Numbers & Websites, later in this chapter.) If you're a member of Zipcar, the large American car-sharing service, you'll find several depots in the downtown core.

Getting **There**

By Plane
Toronto's main airport, and Canada's busiest, is the Toronto Pearson International Airport (☎ 866/207-1690; www.gtaa.com), known simply as Pearson. A taxi will get you from any of its three terminals to downtown in approximately 30 minutes, depending on traffic. The airport authority licenses taxis and limousines that serve Pearson to ensure fair, consistent rates. The flat rate for a one-way downtown trip is $50.

Cheaper methods include the Pacific Western Airport Express (☎ 800/387-6787; www.toronto

airportexpress.com), which runs regular, comfortable buses to and from several major hotels. The fare is $20 one-way. GO Transit (☎ 416/869-3200; www.gotransit.com), the commuter rail service, operates buses from Yorkdale and York Mills subway stations every hour and the trips take 35 and 45 minutes respectively. The fare is $4.45 one-way. The Toronto Transit Commission's (☎ 416/393-4636; www.ttc.ca) 192 Airport Rocket bus route connects Pearson to the Kipling subway stop (about 20 min.). It's the most inexpensive option with a fare of $3 one-way, but the buses are generally crowded and inconvenient if you're carrying a lot of luggage. Aside from commuter and charter services, Porter Airlines (☎ 888/619-8622; www.flyporter.com) is the only commercial airliner that flies out of the Toronto Island Airport, located a short ferry ride from the foot of Bathurst Street. Porter's increasingly popular flights offer short-haul service to Chicago, New York, Montreal, Halifax, and Ottawa, among other locations.

By Car
There are multiple ways to get to Toronto from the U.S. The most popular include the I-75 from Michigan (entering at Detroit-Windsor) and the I-90 from upstate New York (entering from Buffalo or Niagara Falls). From there, make your way to Hwy. 401 or Hwy. 2 and the Queen Elizabeth Way, all of which get you into the city. Coming from the east via Montreal, you'll take the same highways.

Toronto is about 155km (96 miles) from Buffalo, 379km (235 miles) from Detroit, and 545km (339 miles) from Montreal.

By Train
The Maple Leaf line, operated jointly by Amtrak (☎ 800/872-7245; www.amtrak.com) and VIA Rail (☎ 888/842-7245; www.viarail.ca), runs from New York City to Toronto, with stops in Albany, Buffalo, and Niagara Falls. The trip's just over 12 hours, but can be surprisingly pleasant. (Less pleasant are the customs and immigration checks at the border crossing.) Trains arrive in Toronto at Union Station (65 Front St. W.), across the street from the Fairmont Royal York Hotel.

By Bus
Greyhound (☎ 800/231-2222; www.greyhound.com) operates the only bus service from the U.S. into Canada. The main bus terminal is conveniently located near the Eaton Centre, at 610 Bay St. (just north of Dundas).

Getting **Around**

By Public Transportation
Affectionately called the Red Rocket by some locals, the Better Way by the city, and the Bitter Way by disgruntled locals fed up with its inconsistent service, the Toronto Transit Commission (TTC; ☎ 416/393-4636; www.ttc.ca) is the city's network of buses, streetcars, and subways. It's generally a good service and very affordable. Once you figure out its nuances (and how to ignore the odd cranky driver), it'll get you where you want to go with surprising efficiency. A single fare is $3, including transfers to buses and streetcars. Students ages 13 to 19, with valid ID, as well as seniors, pay $2. Children 11 and under pay 75¢. You can buy a day pass for $10 or a weekly pass for $36, both of which allow you unlimited travel on the entire TTC system. On surface transportation, you need a ticket, token, pass,

or exact change. You can buy tickets, tokens, and passes at all subway stops or at authorized stores that display signs advertising TTC tickets. If you plan to transfer between subways or buses or streetcars, you must obtain your free transfer where you board. In the subway, machines dispense these just inside the entrance. On buses or streetcars, just ask the driver.

The subway consists of two major lines—the north-south U-shaped Yonge-University-Spadina and the east-west Bloor-Danforth—and a smaller, newer line, Sheppard, at the northern edge of the city. A small LRT (Light Rapid Transit) line runs along Queens Quay to Spadina Avenue, connecting Union Station to Harbourfront. Hours of operation are Monday to Saturday 6am to 1:30am and Sunday 9am to 1:30am. The Blue Night Network, a special line of all-night buses and streetcars, operates on main routes from 1am to 5:30am. Look for the special reflective blue bands on bus shelter poles.

Buses and streetcars crisscross the city, running in all directions. Car traffic can affect their timeliness, but schedules are posted at shelter stops and, depending on the time of day, vehicles usually come along every 5 to 15 minutes. The TTC website provides real-time schedules as well.

By Taxi

Taxicabs in Toronto charge by the kilometer and the minute, according to a rate regulated by the city. Fares are standard, non-negotiable, and metered. As of press time, fares start at $4 for the first .155km (.096 mile) and each additional .155km (.096 mile) or 31 seconds of engagement time is 25¢. You can find

cabs easily on major streets or in front of big hotels or you can call Toronto Taxi (☎ 416/829-4222 [TAX-ICAB]), Beck (☎ 416/751-5555), Diamond (☎ 416/366-6868), or Co-op (☎ 416/504-2667).

By Car

Driving in Toronto is straightforward. In downtown, the city's grid system is easy enough to navigate, although traffic can be a nightmare (ditto for the highways and expressways leading in and out of the city). As with many cities struggling with growing pains, there's low-simmering tension between drivers, pedestrians, and a growing number of cyclists. If you're driving during the warmer months, be aware that some major arteries also have bike lanes and that cyclists can creep up on your right-hand side. You can turn right on most red lights, although a handful of intersections (notably Yonge and Bloor) prohibit this. Parking can be a nuisance, but keep your eyes peeled for the cheaper Green P lots (obvious from their green signs), administered by the Toronto Parking Authority (TPA)—there are about 160 lots in the city. The TPA also operates approximately 17,500 metered street parking spaces ($1–$3/hr.). Rates are always posted on the meter.

By Foot

If you can, get out and walk. Toronto's very flat city, for the most part, and extremely safe. You'll see a lot more, of course, and discover things you didn't even know were there. During the summer, a few small streets—Baldwin Street, Mirvish Village, and parts of Kensington Market—are actually closed to traffic. As part of Pedestrian Sundays, these several blocks are transformed, temporarily, into car-free carnivals.

Fast **Facts**

APARTMENT RENTALS The most efficient and popular rental service is **View It** (☎ 877/843-9487; www.viewit.ca), which features extensive photos and detailed listings. Another good resource is **www.torontorentals.com**, and it also includes listings for Stratford and other Ontario cities.

ATMS/CASHPOINTS Bank cards that use the **Cirrus** (☎ 800/424-7787; www.mastercard.com) and **PLUS** (☎ 800/843-7587) networks are accepted at all ATMs in Toronto. All banks contain ATMs (although access to them is sometimes available only during banking hours) and several convenience stores do as well. Beware that the convenience store ATMs, unless affiliated with a Canadian bank, are privately owned and operated and the transaction fees can be much higher than those at bank ATMs.

BABYSITTERS Many hotels offer child-care services. Another option is **Christopher Robin** (☎ 416/483-4744; www.christopherrobin.homestead.com), a team of accredited, international babysitters that's been in business since 1953.

BUSINESS HOURS Most banks are open Monday to Friday from 8:00am to 4pm (Thurs–Fri until 5pm) with some branches open Saturday 9:30am to 4pm. Most offices are open Monday through Friday 9am to 5pm. Shops are typically open Monday through Saturday from 10am to 6pm with many open until 8pm on Thursday and Friday. Sunday hours are typically abbreviated, usually from noon until 5 or 6pm, but some stores are closed on Sunday, a holdover from when shopping was banned entirely on Sunday. Big malls like the Eaton Centre generally stay open later, until 9pm during the week. Many restaurants are closed on Monday.

CONSULATES & EMBASSIES All embassies are located in Ottawa, the national capital, but Toronto consulates include the **Australian Consulate General,** 175 Bloor St. E., Ste. 1100 South Tower (☎ 416/323-1155); **British Consulate-General,** 777 Bay St., Ste. 2800 (☎ 416/593-1290); and the **U.S. Consulate,** 360 University Ave. (☎ 416/955-1700).

CURRENCY EXCHANGE You can exchange currency or traveler's checks at currency-exchange shops or hotels, but you'll get the best rates at banks. Check current rates before your trip at **www.xe.com/ucc**.

CUSTOMS Canada is not terribly restrictive when it comes to bringing in typical personal possessions. There are restrictions, however, for alcohol, tobacco products, and firearms. Travelers 18 and over can bring in 200 cigarettes or 50 cigars and 1.14L of spirits, 1.5L of wine, or 24 bottles or cans of beer. Nonrestricted firearms—sporting rifles or shotguns—can be imported for sport, competition, or hunting. For more detailed information, contact the **Canada Customs Office** (☎ 800/461-9999; www.cbsa-asfc.gc.ca).

DENTISTS & DOCTORS See "Emergencies," below.

ELECTRICITY Like the United States, Canada uses 110 volts, 60 cycles AC. You'll need a voltage transformer/converter for your electrical appliances if they operate on a different voltage.

EMERGENCIES For general emergencies, call ☎ **911** for fire, police, or an ambulance. For emergency dentists, the front-desk staff at your hotel should be able to recommend one, or call the **Dental Emergency Service** (☎ **416/485-7121**). The hotel staff or concierge should also be able to locate a doctor for you. Otherwise, call the **College of Physicians and Surgeons of Ontario** (☎ **416/967-2600**) for a referral from 8am to 5pm Monday through Friday.

EVENTS For comprehensive, up-to-the-minute event listings, check both *Now* (www.nowtoronto.com) and *Eye* (www.eyeweekly.com), free alternative weeklies found in boxes, bars, and restaurants all over the city. *Toronto Life* (www.torontolife.com) is a monthly city magazine that offers more detailed listings. *Xtra* (www.xtra.ca) is a free, biweekly newspaper, also available in boxes (they're purple) around the city, that caters to the gay and lesbian community. *Exclaim* (www.exclaim.ca) is a free monthly music paper, with much of its content devoted to local bands and events. Also see Festivals & Special Events, p 162.

GAY & LESBIAN TRAVELERS Toronto's gay and lesbian population is reportedly the third largest in the world and gay and lesbian travelers will feel safe and welcome in the city. The so-called Gay Village, with its many shops, restaurants, and bars, is located along the blocks north and south of Church and Wellesley Streets (this is also the center of Pride festivities). Of course, many gays and lesbians live all over the city, largely in the neighborhoods of West Queen West (dubbed, affectionately, "West

Queer West"), Riverdale, and Leslieville. Same-sex marriage has been permitted in Canada since 2003 and couples can obtain licenses from any municipal office for $130. The website, www.gaytorontotourism.com provides abundant information about the city for gay travelers.

HOLIDAYS Public holidays include New Year's Day (Jan 1), Family Day (third Mon in Feb), Good Friday (Fri before Easter Sunday), Easter Monday (Mon following Good Friday, only for federal employees), Victoria Day (Mon before May 25), Canada Day (July 1), Simcoe Day (first Mon in Aug), Labor Day (first Mon in Sept), Thanksgiving Day (second Mon in Oct), Christmas Day (Dec 25), and Boxing Day (Dec 26).

INSURANCE Check your existing insurance policies (especially with credit cards) before you purchase extra insurance to cover trip cancellation, lost luggage, medical expenses, or car-rental insurance. The cost of travel insurance varies widely, depending on the destination, the cost and length of your trip, your age and health, and the type of trip you're taking. You can get estimates from various providers through **InsureMyTrip.com**. Enter your trip cost and dates, your age, and other information, for prices from more than a dozen companies.

Medical Insurance: Most U.S. health plans do not provide coverage outside of the U.S., and the ones that do often require you to pay for services upfront and reimburse you only after you return home. As a safety net, you may want to buy travel medical insurance from providers like **MEDEX Assistance** (☎ **410/453-6300**; www.medexassist.com) or **Travel Assistance International** (☎ **800/821-2828**; www.travelassistance.com).

Trip-Cancellation Insurance:
Trip-cancellation insurance typically covers you if you have to back out of a trip (due to illness, for example), if your travel supplier goes bankrupt, if there's a natural disaster, or if your government advises against travel to your destination—which isn't much of a worry for Toronto. Some plans cover cancellations for any reason. **TravelSafe** (☎ **888/885-7233;** www.travelsafe.com) offers both types of coverage. **Expedia** (www.expedia.com) also offers any-reason cancellation coverage for its air-hotel packages. Other recommended insurers include **Access America** (☎ **866/807-3982;** www.accessamerica.com), **Travel Guard International** (☎ **800/826-4919;** www.travelguard.com), **Travel Insured International** (☎ **800/243-3174;** www.travelinsured.com), and **Travelex Insurance Services** (☎ **888/457-4602;** www.travelex-insurance.com).

Lost-Luggage Insurance: If your airline loses your luggage, immediately file a lost-luggage claim at the airport, detailing the luggage contents. Most airlines require that you report delayed, damaged, or lost baggage within 4 hours of arrival. On international flights, baggage coverage is limited to approximately $10 per pound, up to approximately $700 per checked bag. If you plan to check items more valuable than what's covered by the standard liability, see if your homeowner's policy covers your valuables, or get baggage insurance as part of your comprehensive travel-insurance package.

INTERNET Just about every Toronto hotel now provides dataports or Wi-Fi access (often, increasingly, in guest rooms). Coffee shops and cafes, more often than not, also offer free Internet access. If you don't have your own computer or smartphone, you can try the pleasant **Net Effect Internet Café,** 9 Isabella St., 2nd Floor (☎ **416/964-0749**), centrally located and open 24 hours a day.

LIQUOR The minimum drinking age is 19. Bar hours are daily from 11am to 2am (though these are extended for designated bars during special occasions like the Toronto International Film Festival and Scotiabank Nuit Blanche). Alcohol is only available at government-operated retail outlets scattered throughout the city. The **Liquor Control Board of Ontario** (LCBO) stores sell liquor, wine, and several kinds of beer and are open daily from 10am to 6pm (Sun noon–5pm), although many are open into the evening. Visit www.lcbo.com for locations and hours. Beer is also available at the **Beer Store** (www.thebeerstore.ca). Its many locations are generally open daily from 10am to 9pm (Sun noon–5pm).

LOST PROPERTY As anywhere, call your credit card company immediately if your wallet or purse has been lost or stolen, and file a police report at the nearest precinct (see "Police," below). Items lost on the subway, bus, or streetcar can be retrieved at the **TTC Lost Articles Office** (☎ **416/393-4100**). It's located at the Bay Street subway station, and is open Monday to Friday from 8am to 5pm.

MAIL & POSTAGE At press time, postage for a letter (up to 30g/about 1 oz.) to the United States cost 98¢; international letters cost $1.65. Mailing letters within Canada costs 54¢. Postcards cost the same as a letter.

Postal services are available at many convenience stores and drugstores. (Look for the red-white-and-blue Canada Post signage.) Actual post offices are scattered throughout the city as well; check with **Canada Post** (☎ 416/979-8822; www.canadapost.ca).

MONEY Canadian currency comes in graduated, multicolored denominations of dollars and cents. The dollar and two-dollar exist only as coins, called the Loonie (because of the picture of a loon engraved on it) and Toonie (pronounced "two-knee") respectively. At press time, the Canadian dollar was worth 92¢ in U.S. currency and 56p in U.K. currency. Credit and debit cards are accepted at virtually every shop, hotel, and restaurant in the city, but having some cash on hand is wise.

NEWSPAPERS AND MAGAZINES The city's major newspapers are the **Toronto Star** and the tabloid **Toronto Sun**, although both national newspapers, the **Globe and Mail** and the **National Post,** are well-read here and have large local sections. (See "Events," above for other free arts-and-entertainment weeklies.) On the subway or in boxes around the city, you can pick up the free, digestlike **Metro** newspaper. The city's preeminent monthly magazine is **Toronto Life,** available at all newsstands and convenience stores. **Where Toronto** is an events guide that's usually found free at hotels.

PASSPORTS Every visitor to Canada needs a passport to enter the country, including people arriving from the United States. Visas are required only of selected nationals (visit the Citizenship and Immigration Canada website at www.cic.gc.ca for the list). If your passport is lost or stolen, contact your country's consulate immediately (see "Consulates & Embassies," above).

POLICE Call ☎ **911** for police. Toronto Police Services precincts are called Divisions and can be located by calling ☎ **416/808-2222** or visiting www.torontopolice.on.ca.

SAFETY As large cities go, Toronto is very safe, but exercise the same caution you'd use in any urban center. Violent crime remains rare downtown, but it's best to avoid the larger parks at night. The Entertainment District on a weekend night can, at times, become overcrowded and dangerous, hence the large police presence and mounted cameras.

SENIOR TRAVELERS Travelers 66 years of age and over are usually entitled to discounts in many, if not all, Toronto museums, theaters, and attractions, as well as on the TTC. Many hotels also offer discounts to seniors.

SMOKING Outside of private homes, you can't smoke in any enclosed place in Ontario. You can smoke on patios of restaurants and bars provided they're not covered. In 2009, Ontario became the third province in Canada to enact legislation to ban smoking in cars when children are present.

TAXES The general provincial retail sales tax is 8%. On accommodations, it's 5%; on admission of more than $4 to places of amusement, it's 10%; for alcohol at licensed establishments, it's 10%. There is an additional 5% national goods-and-services tax (GST), and at press time, the Ontario government had proposed harmonizing these two taxes into a single 13% tax starting in 2010. Books, feminine hygiene products, and children's clothing are exempt from the province's portion of the tax.

TELEPHONES   The telephone system, operated by Bell Canada, is very similar to the one in the U.S. A local call from a pay phone (increasingly difficult to find but usually located near major intersections) costs 50¢. The United States and Canada are on the same long-distance system. Canada's international prefix is 1.

TIPPING   Gratuities operate the same as in any North American city: 15%–20% in restaurants, 10%–15% in taxis, $1 per bag for hotel porters and valets, and $1–$2 per day for hotel cleaning staff.

TOILETS   Public bathrooms are rare, although they can be found in larger parks and all amusement and big tourist areas. While some restaurants and cafes only allow customers to use their bathrooms, it's usually easy to find one that will look kindly upon a tourist in need. Coffee chains like Starbucks, Second Cup, and Tim Horton's are good bets.

TOURS   Several tour operators offer city orientation and special-interest tours. **Toronto Tours** (☎ 416/869-1372; www.torontotours.com) is the oldest in town and offers city tours, trips around the harbor and

islands, or all the way to Niagara Falls. The **Gray Line Hop-On Hop-Off City Tour** (☎ 800/594-3310; www.grayline.ca) is a 2-hour bus tour offering exactly what the name suggests, the ability to get on and off whenever you like. The whimsical **Toronto Hippo Tours** (☎ 877/635-5510; www.torontohippotours.com) takes travelers around town (and water) in an amphibious hippo-shaped bus. Why a hippo and not a more culturally appropriate beaver? Who knows.

TRAVELERS WITH DISABILITIES
Toronto's pretty good for travelers with disabilities—sidewalks have curb cuts and increasing numbers of businesses and restaurants have wheelchair ramps. About a third of the subway stations have elevators and the TTC now has more than 1,400 accessible buses running on more than 125 routes. These buses have low floors and are equipped with a flip ramp and kneeling feature. They have blue lights on either side of the front destination sign and the blue international wheelchair symbol above the front right bumper. All fully accessible buses include two wheelchair/scooter positions.

Toronto: **A Brief History**

1635 Etienne Brulé travels the Toronto Trail. Despite popular misconceptions that *Toronto* is a Huron term for "meeting place," it's actually derived from a Mohawk phrase meaning "trees standing in water."

1720 France establishes an outpost at Toronto.

1751 The French build Fort Rouillé.

1759 Fort Rouillé burns during the British conquest.

1763 The Treaty of Paris ends French rule in Canada.

1787 Lord Dorchester, British governor of Quebec, purchases 1,000sq. km (386 sq. miles) of what is present-day Toronto from the Mississauga tribe.

1793 Col. John Simcoe, governor of Upper Canada, arrives and names the settlement York. It becomes the capital of Upper Canada.

1812–1815 Canada becomes a battleground as the U.S. and England fight the War of 1812. In 1813, Americans invade, blow up Fort York, and burn Parliament buildings. In 1814, U.S. troops are expelled from Canada.

1832–1834 Cholera epidemics ravage the population.

1834 The city is named Toronto; William Lyon Mackenzie becomes the first mayor.

1837 Former mayor Mackenzie leads a rebellion sparked by an economic downturn.

1841 Act of Union establishes the United Province of Canada, with Kingston as ruling seat; Toronto loses status as the capital.

1843 King's College opens.

1844 City Hall is built. George Brown founds the *Globe* newspaper.

1849 Fire destroys much of the city. Anglican King's College converts to the secular University of Toronto.

1851 The population reaches 30,000 (33% Irish). St. Lawrence Hall is built.

1852 The Toronto Stock Exchange opens.

1853 St. James' Cathedral is completed. The first trains pull out of Toronto.

1858 A storm creates the Toronto Islands.

1867 The Canadian Confederation is created; Toronto becomes the capital of the new province of Ontario.

1869 Eaton's department store opens.

1871 The population reaches 56,000.

1886 Provincial parliament buildings are erected in Queen's Park.

1893 The first Stanley Cup is played.

1896 *Maclean's* magazine begins publication.

1900 The Art Gallery of Toronto (later Ontario) is founded.

1901 The population is 208,000.

1904 The Great Fire burns much of downtown.

1906 The Toronto Symphony is founded.

1907 The Royal Alexandra Theatre opens. The Lord's Day Act prohibits all public activity except churchgoing on Sunday.

1912 The Royal Ontario Museum is founded.

1914 The New Union Station is built.

1914–1918 World War I is waged; 70,000 Torontonians enlist; 13,000 perish.

1920 The Art Gallery of Toronto mounts the first Group of Seven exhibit.

1921 The population is 521,893.

1922 University of Toronto researchers Frederick Banting and Charles Best discover insulin.

1923 Frederick Banting is awarded the Nobel Prize in Medicine. Parliament passes the Chinese Exclusion Act. Ernest Hemingway moves to Toronto to become reporter for the *Star*.

1931 Maple Leaf Gardens is built as a home base for the Maple Leafs.

1933 The Christie Pits Riot, the largest in the city's history, pits Jews, then the largest minority, against anti-Semitic Protestants.

1938 Toronto native Joseph Shuster cocreates *Superman* with Cleveland friend Jerry Siegel.

1939 Canada enters World War II.

1947 The Chinese Exclusion Act is repealed. Cocktail lounges are approved.

1949 Construction begins on "Canada's First Subway," the beginnings of the TTC's subway system.

1950 The Lord's Day Act is amended to permit sports—except horse racing—to be played on Sundays.

1951 Thirty-one percent of the population is foreign born.

1954 Hurricane Hazel kills 83 people in Toronto.

1959 York University, Toronto's second major institution of higher education, opens.

1960 Movies are shown on Sunday for the first time.

1961 Forty-two percent of the population is foreign born.

1963 Ryerson Polytechnic University is founded.

1965 The new City Hall at Nathan Phillips Square opens. Canada and the U.S. sign the Autopact, creating boom times in Toronto and nearby Oshawa.

1966 The province consolidates the 13 municipalities that made up Metro Toronto into one City of Toronto and five boroughs (including Etobicoke and Scarborough); The Art Gallery of Toronto becomes the Art Gallery of Ontario.

1967 The Maple Leafs win the Stanley Cup.

1969 Urbanist Jane Jacobs moves from New York to Toronto's Annex neighborhood.

1970 An influx of immigration from Asia, Africa, India, Pakistan, the Caribbean, and Latin America occurs.

1971 Construction of controversial Spadina Expressway is halted.

1976 The Festival of Festivals (later the Toronto International Film Festival) is founded. CN Tower opens, then the world's largest freestanding structure on land.

1980s The Greater Toronto Area (GTA) is formed, including nearby cities of Mississauga, Oshawa, and Burlington.

1981 The population of the GTA is 3,898,933.

1984 The city's 150th anniversary.

1989 The SkyDome opens, drawing wide criticism for its $570-million cost.

1992 The Blue Jays win their first World Series.

1993 The Blue Jays win their second World Series.

1995 The NBA expands into Canada, and the Toronto Raptors is established.

1996 The population of the GTA is 4,263,757. University of Toronto professor John Polanyi wins the Nobel Prize in Chemistry.

1997 Protests arise over Bill 103, which would bring together the old City of Toronto and six municipalities (including North York and Scarborough) into a single "megacity."

1998 Toronto becomes a megacity, the fifth largest in North America.

1999 The last game is played at Maple Leaf Gardens; the new Air Canada Centre becomes home to the Leafs and the Raptors.

2002 Toronto hosts the first World Youth Day ever held in Canada; Pope John Paul II visits.

2003 Tourism drops due to the SARS scare. Same-sex marriage is legalized in Ontario in June. The largest blackout in North American history hits Toronto, lasting several days in some areas.

2006 The long-awaited Four Seasons Centre for the Performing Arts, Toronto's new opera house, opens. The GTA population reaches 5,113,149.

2007 The Royal Ontario Museum unveils the Michael Lee-Chin Crystal, designed by Daniel Libeskind.

2008 The Art Gallery of Ontario reopens after major redesign by native son Frank Gehry.

Toll-Free Numbers & Websites

Airlines

AER LINGUS
☎ 800/474-7424
    in the U.S.
☎ 01/886-8888
    in Ireland
www.aerlingus.com

AIR CANADA
☎ 888/247-2262
www.aircanada.com

AIR FRANCE
☎ 0820/820-820
    in France
www.airfrance.com

AIR NEW ZEALAND
☎ 800/262-1234
    in New Zealand
www.airnewzealand.com

AMERICAN AIRLINES
☎ 800/433-7300
www.aa.com

BRITISH AIRWAYS
☎ 800/247-9297 or
    ☎ 0345/222-1111
☎ 0845/77-333-77
    in Britain
www.british-airways.com

CONTINENTAL AIRLINES
☎ 800/525-0280
www.continental.com

DELTA AIR LINES
☎ 800/221-1212
www.delta.com

NORTHWEST AIRLINES
☎ 800/225-2525
www.nwa.com

PORTER AIRLINES
☎ 888/619-8622
www.flyporter.com

QANTAS
☎ 800/227-4500
    in the U.S.
☎ 612/131313
    in Australia
www.qantas.com

UNITED AIRLINES
☎ 800/241-6522
www.united.com

US AIRWAYS
☎ 800/428-4322
www.usairways.com

WEST JET
☎ 888/937-8538
www.westjet.com

Car Rental Agencies

ALAMO
☎ 877-222-9075
www.alamo.com

AVIS
☎ 800/879-2847
www.avis.com

BUDGET
☎ 800/268-8900
www.budget.com

DOLLAR
☎ 800/800-3665
www.dollar.com

ENTERPRISE
☎ 800/325-8007
www.enterprise.com

HERTZ
☎ 800/263-0600
www.hertz.com

NATIONAL
☎ 877-222-9058
www.nationalcar.com

THRIFTY
☎ 800/847-4389
www.thrifty.com

Hotel & Motel Chains

BEST WESTERN INTERNATIONAL
☎ 800/528-1234
www.bestwestern.com

COMFORT INNS
☎ 800/228-5150
www.comfortinn.com

DAYS INN
☎ 800/325-2525
www.daysinn.com

DELTA HOTELS & RESORTS
☎ 877/814-7706
www.deltahotels.com

FAIRMONT HOTELS
☎ 800/257-7544
www.fairmont.com

FOUR SEASONS
☎ 800/819-5053
www.fourseasons.com

HILTON HOTELS
☎ 800/HILTONS (445-8667)
www.hilton.com

HOLIDAY INN
☎ 800/HOLIDAY (465-4329)
www.ichotelsgroup.com

HOWARD JOHNSON
☎ 800/654-2000
www.hojo.com

HYATT HOTELS & RESORTS
☎ 800/228-9000
www.hyatt.com

MARRIOTT HOTELS
☎ 800/228-9290
www.marriott.com

RADISSON HOTELS INTERNATIONAL
☎ 800/333-3333
www.radisson.com

RITZ-CARLTON
☎ 800/241-3333
www.ritzcarlton.com

SHERATON HOTELS & RESORTS
☎ 800/325-3535
www.sheraton.com

WESTIN HOTELS & RESORTS
☎ 800/937-8461
www.westin.com

Toll-Free Numbers & Websites

Index

See also Accommodations and Restaurant indexes, below.

Photo **Credits**

p viii: © Liz Sullivan; p 4: © Liz Sullivan; p 5, top: © Peter Spiro/istockphoto; p 5, bottom: © Liz Sullivan; p 6, top: © Nathan Denette/CP Photo; p 6, bottom: © Pete Nema (petenema. com); p 7: © Chris Cheadle/All Canada Photos; p 9, top: Royal Ontario Museum © 2008. All rights reserved; p 9, bottom: © Liz Sullivan; p 10: © Liz Sullivan; p 11: © Monica Wells/PCL Travel; p 13, top: © Klaus Lang/All Canada Photos; p 13, bottom: © Chris Cheadle/All Canada Photos; p 14: © Chris Cheadle/All Canada Photos; p 15: © Monica Wells/PCL Travel; p 18: © Bouke Salverde; p 19, top: © Liz Sullivan; p 19, bottom: © Henry Georgi/All Canada Photos; p 20: © Rolf Hicker/All Canada Photos; p 21: © Liz Sullivan; p 23, top: © Courtesy Gardiner Museum Toronto; p 23, bottom: Royal Ontario Museum © 2008. All rights reserved; p 24: Cherokee Mocassin, c. 1840. On view in 'Beauty, Identity, Pride: Native North American Footwear' at the Bata Shoe Museum © 2009 Bata Shoe Museum (photo: Matthew Plexman); p 25: © Apr 7 09 - Yaniw Stavreva - A Chandra/Four Seasons Centre; p 26: © Young Centre exterior. Photo: Tom Arban; p 27, top: © Liz Sullivan; p 27, bottom: © Cat O'Neil; p 30: © Robin Sharp (sharp-photo.com); p 31: © Courtesy Anne Freeman/ Dufferin Grove Organic Farmers' Market; p 32, top: © Robin Sharp (sharp-photo.com); p 32, bottom: © Liz Sullivan; p 33: © Liz Sullivan; p 35: © Courtesy Ontario Science Centre; p 36: Royal Ontario Museum © 2008. All rights reserved; p 37: © Liz Sullivan; p 38: © Jane Miller as Lucy, Photo: Daniel Alexander; p 39, top: © Liz Sullivan; p 39, bottom: © Liz Sullivan; p 41: © Richard Johnson, interiorimages.ca/Sharp Centre for Design, at the Ontario College of Art & Design; p 42: © Liz Sullivan; p 43: © Liz Sullivan; p 44, top: © Courtesy Katherine Mulherin Contemporary Art Projects; p 44, bottom: © Tom Arban/The Museum of Inuit Art; p 45: © Thrush Holmes, EVERY OLD VERSE, 2008, mixed media with neon lights on panel, Dorian Fitzgerald Gabana Yacht, 2008, acrylic & caulking on canvas/ MOCCA; p 47: © PCL/Alamy; p 48: © Liz Sullivan; p 49, top: © Stephen Finn/Alamy; p 49, bottom: © Vast Photography/agefotostock; p 51: © Courtesy City of Toronto; p 52: © Courtesy The Santa Claus Parade, Toronto, Photographer: Michael Grills; p 53: © Courtesy Anne Freeman/ Dufferin Grove Organic Farmers' Market; p 55: © Robin Sharp (sharp-photo.com); p 56: © Liz Sullivan; p 57, top: © Liz Sullivan; p 57, bottom: © Courtesy Holt Renfrew; p 59, top: © Courtesy Wynick Tuck Gallery; p 59, bottom: © Courtesy of MuchMusic; p 60: © Liz Sullivan; p 61: © Cecilia Berkovic; p 63: © Liz Sullivan; p 64: © Liz Sullivan; p 65, top: © Liz Sullivan; p 65, bottom: © Robin Sharp (sharp-photo. com); p 67: © Liz Sullivan; p 68: © Liz Sullivan; p 69, top: © Liz Sullivan; p 69, bottom: © Liz Sullivan; p 71: © Robin Sharp (sharp-photo.com); p 72: © Liz Sullivan; p 73, top: © Robin Sharp (sharp-photo.com); p 73, bottom: © Hisham Ibrahim/PhotoV/Alamy; p 75: © Robin Sharp (sharp-photo.com); p 76: © Robin Sharp (sharp-photo.com); p 80: © Robin Sharp (sharp-photo.com); p 81: © Courtesy Type Books, Toronto; p 82: © Robin Sharp (sharp-photo. com); p 83: © Courtesy Holt Renfrew; p 84: © Jennifer Rowsom; p 85: © Courtesy Design Within Reach, Toronto; p 86, top: © Courtesy Studio Brillantine, Toronto; p 86, bottom: © Candice Craig for Sparklypear Design; p 87: © Oleksiy Maksymenko/All Canada Photos; p 88: © Burdifilek; p 89: © Chris Cheadle/All Canada Photos; p 91, top: © Liz Sullivan; p 91, bottom: © Liz Sullivan; p 92: © Liz Sullivan; p 93: © Liz Sullivan; p 95: © Liz Sullivan; p 97: © Chris Cheadle/All Canada Photos; p 98: © Courtesty of the Beaches International Jazz Festival; p 99: © Courtesy Bymark Restaurant; p 100: © Courtesy Amuse-Bouche, Toronto; p 104: © Courtesy Amuse-Bouche, Toronto; p 105: © Courtesy Bymark Restaurant; p 106: © Courtesy Colborne Lane Restaurant & Bar; p 107, top: © Photo by Aaron Phelan/ Drake Hotel; p 107, bottom: © Courtesy Fresh; p 109: © Courtesy of ki modern japanese and bar; p 110: © Courtesy Magic Oven Pizza; p 111, top: © Courtesy One Restaurant; p 111, bottom: © Robin Sharp (sharp-photo.com); p 112: © Robin Sharp (sharp-photo.com); p 113:

Frommer's 500 Places

These destination-packed global guides bring together practical travel information and armchair inspiration into one irresistible package.

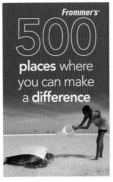

New from Frommer's!

See the world by walking with Frommer's Best Hiking Trips!

Frommer's

Best Hiking Trips in
Northern California

With 60 great hikes, plus where to eat and stay

With full-color wildlife guide

Frommer's

Best Walking Trips in
Scotland

With 57 walks, plus where to eat and stay

With full-color wildlife guide

Frommer's

Best Hiking Trips in
Northern California

With 60 great hikes, plus where to eat and stay

With full-color wildlife guide

Frommer's

Best Hiking Trips in
Hawaii

With 60 great hikes, plus where to eat and stay

With full-color wildlife guide

Every book comes with innovative features and great resources in the Frommer's style:

- Two-color maps for every route
- Accommodation and restaurant reviews for businesses close to the trails
- A full-color introduction and wildlife identification guide
- GPS coordinates for every trailhead and waypoint